BROOKLYN
WRITERS PRESS

Copyright 2025 by Jere Pfister

All rights reserved.

Published in the United States of America by the Brooklyn Writers Press, an imprint of Book Biz Hub, LLC
brooklynwriterspress.com

Brooklyn Writers Press values and supports copyright. Copyright fuels creativity, encourages diverse voices, promotes freedom of expression, and supports a vibrant culture. Thank you for purchasing an authorized edition of this book and for respecting intellectual property laws by not reproducing, scanning, or distributing any part of it by any means without permission. You are supporting authors and enabling the Brooklyn Writers Press to continue to publish books for everyone. No part of this book may be used or reproduced in any manner for the purpose of training artificial intelligence technologies or systems.

In accordance with Article 4(3) of the Digital Single Market Directive 2019/790, the Brooklyn Writers Press expressly reserves this work from the text and data mining exception.

For permissions or information on bulk orders, please contact:
publish@bklynwriterspress.com

ISBNs:
978-1-952991-48-6 (e-Book)
978-1-952991-49-3 (Paperback)
978-1-952991-50-9 (Hardback)

Library of Congress No. 2025916457

First Edition

Cover design by the Brooklyn Writers Press

Printed in the United States of America

Contents

Author's Note	v
1. Diggin' up the Dead	1
2. The House on Military Road	4
3. The Chicken Coop	12
4. Caregivers	16
5. Easter Sunday	24
6. The Power of Story	28
7. The Powers that Be (Part 1)	34
8. The Powers that Be (Part 2)	46
9. Fisherwoman	60
10. Ruby	63
11. San Juan Ranch	65
12. Good Mothers	73
13. Good Sisters	80
14. The Turn of the Screw	90
15. Trying On Bad	96
16. Return to the South	107
17. Mama's Opus	119
18. Mama (Part 1)	130
19. No More Letters	144
20. Mama (Part 2)	151
21. The Alone Years	155
22. Michigan	163
23. A Horrid Death	172
24. The Making of A Ghost	177
25. Flashback	199
26. The Rhine River	200

27. The Eclipse 206
    Epilogue 220

    About the Author 223

Author's Note

I have written this memoir over several years, from the late 90s until shortly after Hurricane Katrina.

I was born in early 1941 and, for whatever reason, my memory stretches back to my second year. I have written a great deal of dialogue inside these pages because that is how I think and because I am a playwright. And of course, because comic books with their illustrations and dialogue and storyline were part and parcel of my early years. And I talk a lot as I hold conversations with myself and others. I am an extrovert and a keen observer. Though this book covers many years, it is not an autobiography. It is a map to falling in love with self and others.

Some readers may be disturbed by the vernacular of an earlier time and place. It is racist and hateful. But sad to say it is still prevalent throughout our country, and erasing it will not make it go away. But we try.

Where possible, I have used more acceptable language.

CHAPTER 1

Diggin' up the Dead

Sometimes, death comes on the wind. In 1948, when I was seven years old, I awakened to the sound of a squeaky wheelbarrow. It was early morning, and my father was walking alongside the country boy he hired on occasion. Our house was on a highway where our dogs were no match for the speeding cars and trucks. That morning, a large, black cocker spaniel whose name I do not even remember but loved for his gentleness, and his smell of dirt and bad breath, lay dead in the wheelbarrow.

I watched from the upstairs window. My eyes following the men. My ears holding the sound of their voices and the squeak of the wheel. Then I heard the shovel my father had been carrying over his shoulder like a rifle. I stood quietly. Brother awakened and took his place beside me. It was a beautiful sunny Saturday.

As I write these words, my heart hurts in my throat, in the magical place where unreleased tears reside and grow hard inside of us until we cough them up, or perhaps until suddenly and without warning, on a clear day we begin to weep for who knows what. Silence and stillness bring remembrance.

For days after the dog's burial, I waited. Brother kept a close and watchful eye. Then on a cold afternoon when school was out, I finally got a chance to venture into the woods by myself. I waited until everyone was occupied and then slipped away.

I found a sturdy stick I could use to slowly make my way through the thicket. Even though the ground was covered with leaves and dead branches the grave was easy to find. Using my hands and the stick, I dug at the ground. The dog was not buried very deep, so I was able to pull his limp body, heavy with death from the grave and cradle him in my lap.

I do not remember noticing the smell of his rotting flesh until years later when I was in Michigan observing the necropsy of a doe found dead by the road. As the vet cut into its belly, gases released into a cloud that filled my nose, permeated my pores, and moved deep inside my body. It was then I remembered the smell of the dead dog lying in my lap so many years before.

I was suddenly a child again in the woods, my hands black with dirt and dog hair where my brother found me crying and willing my dog alive.

"You can't go around digging up dead things."

"I don't want him to be dead."

"We have to bury him. You'll upset Mother and I'm going to get in trouble for not watching you better. God, you stink."

After, my brother and I held close to the tree line as we made our way down the river. We scrubbed our hands with water and sand and brushed our jackets with pine tree branches. Then he cut some of the grey clay off the cliff and brought it to me. I rubbed the clay between my hands, making snakes which I wound into a spiral. Is it imagination or my wanting it to be so that makes me remember the kindness of an older brother?

When we finally reached the top of the cliff, Mother was standing there, waiting for me and Julian. It was nearly dark when she led us inside to warm ourselves by the big gas heater next to the stairs in the hallway before she served supper. This was the same hallway where Daddy brought us dead game from his early morning hunts, and where we sat with open newspapers around the heater's warmth. It was where Daddy used his knife to cut open small birds, and I would use my small fingers to dig into their stomach and pull out organs that were not good to eat. Dead animals at the table never made me sad. I grieved only what was mine.

CHAPTER 2

The House on Military Road

[1944 - 1949]

Military Road was an old Indian Trail Andrew Jackson followed as he marched his troops to Lake Ponchatrain to meet Jean Lafitte and his pirate ships when they sailed to save the port of New Orleans during the War of 1812. Tall, long-needled pine trees native to the land, along with moss-draped oaks, surround the road.

During my childhood in the 1940s, the curve close to our house was called Dead Man's Curve, and for good reason. It had a dangerous north-south two-lane road with a steep curve. Trucks bearing supplies sped down while passing or running slower moving traffic off the roadway into the clay embankments and drainage ditches.

As you approach the house on Military Road, it seems to stare back at you. Two dormer windows protrude from the sloping roof of the second floor, giving the appearance of eyes. In the very center of the house, the front door and its side windows give the appearance of a nose. And finally, a narrow brick patio runs across the front of the house, like a mouth.

In my childhood, the blooms of miniature gardenia bushes

planted along the patio shone like baby teeth in the spring. Two small concrete elephants stand guard at the entry and front walk.

An enclosed side porch my mother turned into our dining room and my parents' bedroom look like wings on either side of the central house. White paint covers the entire exterior, except for the dark green plank shutters with cross boards at the top and bottom. In the center of the shutters, crescent moon cutouts served as air vents.

Our front and side yards were long-needled pines and one large oak tree. Spring drew a bloom of white blossoms on the flowering magnolias, dogwood, and white bud trees. The filtered light of so many trees made it a haven for the huge azalea bushes that lined the gravel driveway.

Our backyard sat high above the Little Bogue Falaya River, ending at the edge of a twenty-foot cliff of grey clay. Steps carved into the clay led down to the river. Three poisonous Tung oil trees formed a protective boundary, a warning to people the cliff was nearby. The tall pine trees surrounded the small area the sun could reach next to a rose arbor, while providing shade in the rest of the yard. At the end of our long driveway, a gully divided the rest of the backyard.

Short-stemmed pink roses covered the dilapidated wooden rose arbor next to the gully in the spring and summer, where honeybees droned softly. Across the yard was an old, dilapidated chicken coop our father and his helper rebuilt with wire and good intentions for housing for hunting dogs rented by their owners. Whenever my brother and I got close, the loose lipped hounds wailed and slathered spit as they leaped against the fencing.

After church every Sunday, Mama stopped at an icehouse near the railroad tracks on the edge of town. Ruby, our ironing woman, would use the ice Mama bought to make our warm weather ice cream treat. We packed the ice, wrapped it in layers of old newspaper, and placed it into Daddy's old ice chest.

Ruby would emerge from the woods just as Mama was finished cooking our dinner. While the rest of us ate inside, Ruby sat on the back steps and ate the same dinner from an old metal pie dish Mama kept on a shelf over the washing machine on the back porch.

After cleaning the kitchen, it was Ruby's job to set the metal canister Mama filled with ice cream custard into the wooden bucket, to hold it in place, while she chipped the ice and packed it in the canister.

One Sunday, ever helpful, I ran to the shelf in the garage where we stored the rock salt that had to be mixed with the ice to make sure it melted exactly right.

"Hand me the salt, girl."

I hugged the bag of rock salt to my chest.

"No, Ruby, let me put it in. I won't let any salt get in the ice cream. I can do it!"

Without even breaking a beat with her cranking hand, Ruby reached through my tight little arms and dragged the bag away from me.

"Girl, why do you bother me? Go play."

I tried bribery.

"Give me the paddle and I'll go play."

The paddle was the wooden and metal stirrer in the middle of the ice cream canister. Once you removed it, if the ice cream was hard enough, would lend delight to the tongue as we licked the wooden slats that were held together by the metal frame.

My brother, Julian, was three years older than me and could clean off every speck of ice cream before it melted. We had to take turns, and I resented his turn, because it was just another way, he could show off his contempt for me by getting in my face with his superior licking talent.

"Ms. Jere, you know it's your brother's turn to get the paddle today! You just want to stir up a fine mess of yelling and crying and your mama's gonna take your daddy's old belt to your skinny legs. Now you just sit quiet, and I'll slip you something extra."

Thick, black, slimy spit ran down Ruby's face. She took the metal

Band-Aid box she always carried in her breast pocket and spat in it before closing the lid.

"Ruby, you ever spit in our ice cream when nobody's looking?"

She swatted at my exposed flesh with her old wire fly swatter.

"You get, girl, until I call you, and let my ice cream set. And don't you be giving me any of your ideas. I spit lots of places."

As I ran off, Ruby was laughing and talking to herself. Later, I heard Mama's voice calling, "Jere! Jere! Come home!"

When Mama called me back to the house, I was down by the river looking at an old water moccasin sun himself in the shallow depression on the edge of the riverbank.

Everybody else gathered on the back steps already, except Daddy, who really didn't like the dinners Mama cooked. Daddy liked to play games on Sunday afternoons, usually baseball or golf. But this was the summer when he first moved out of our house. Mama tried to make out it didn't bother her, but Brother and I knew it mattered.

Mama was serving the ice cream into bowls. Brother was licking the paddle, getting chocolate ice cream all over his freckled face. He looked at me and smiled, trying to make me mad.

Ruby was already eating her ice cream out of her old tin pie plate. I could see a wad of twisted newspaper sticking up out of the ice in the wood bucket. Ruby had remembered her promise and saved me a kitchen spoon of ice cream. It was all the way down in the ice and would be hard for Ruby to sneak it to me later while Mama took her nap.

While Ruby cleaned the kitchen, I sat on the ladder stool next to the stove and quietly watched her. Everything about her was slow and sad. Curiosity made me stare at her. I must have asked questions about her because in my mind's eye, I can see my mama as she took a long drag of her cigarette as she sipped her coffee. She told me for the umpteenth time that there were two kinds of colored people, good ones and bad ones. And the worst of the bad was uppity.

"Ruby married an uppity man. He took her to Chicago, and they had a baby and there was a race riot." I didn't know what that was. But I knew better than to break my mother's train of thought.

"The Negroes just ask for it, honey. You can't ever move out of your own kind, Jere. It doesn't work. Ruby's husband was uppity. She got all cut up and beaten and he got killed, and so did their baby. And seeing that is how Ruby went crazy. Now don't you go ask her about it or talk about it. You'll make her feel worse and it's not proper, anyway, to go into other people's lives. Do you understand me?"

I wanted to know more about that baby and Ruby's uppity husband. Mama saying not to ask about it was like God putting a tree loaded with beautiful, ripe figs or peaches or apples in the middle of the garden and telling Eve she couldn't eat its fruit.

The story of how Ruby got crazy burned in my brain. It stayed stuck like a fishbone in my heart. But I was obedient about important things, and I knew not asking Ruby about her dead baby was one of them. And like so many mysteries in my childhood, I knew answers would have to wait. I only hoped to live long enough to find the answers I wanted.

So, I busied myself playing outside as much as the weather and Mama allowed. Our backyard was a perfect playground. But the most wonderful place was the gully that ran alongside our backyard. Mama liked being outside as much as Brother and me, at least in the early days of our time on Military Road.

The truth was, Mama did not like the nitty gritty of housework.

"That's what God made colored women for," she would declare to her friends.

My mother always backed up her pronouncements with the name of God. She believed that despite all evidence to the contrary, God had made the world especially for her comfort. And when things didn't go her way, then something was amiss in creation, and she had to work hard to correct it. And that was why Daddy ran off. Maybe she tried to fix him, and he wouldn't fix.

So, like the Creator of us all, our mother planted gardens wherever she lived. The house on Military Road was the perfect landscape for her most spectacular creation.

She planted a garden of succulents and tropical plants in the earth's depression at the end of our long gravel driveway. The indentation of the earth was like a hand closing on itself. When it rained, the gully drained to the river that flowed behind our yard. But it also served as a retention pond. During one hurricane, the river rose so high it lapped at the edge of the cliff that hung over the river and its sandy beach, flooding the gully, but leaving our house dry and safe.

In the magic mind of my childhood, my mother created the gully. My mother lorded over the river and controlled its path as it cut through the woods and alleyways of vegetation and clay earth. My mother caused that river to leave sand so sweet and pure I used it as a kind of soap on my dirty bare feet. But after creating the garden, its lushness frightened her, and she forbade me to enter it alone.

"Jere, don't you go into the gully by yourself. There are snakes down there. Poisonous snakes! You hear me?" Mama had caught me staring down into the garden when I couldn't find my voice or take my eyes away from the lush green.

"Nod your head, then. Those moccasins will bite you and I'll have to take a razor blade and cut the bite open and suck the poison out of your blood. And if I have a cut on my lip, even a little one, I could die. Then wouldn't you feel bad? You would feel guilty all your life for having killed your own mother. You hear me?"

"I hear you, Mama." She stood next to me. She looked down into the gully, looking for whatever I saw.

"What are you looking at?"

"I ain't looking at nothing."

"You are staring. That's what you are doing." Her voice had changed from one of inquiry to suspicion.

"Staring is not lady-like. How are you going to grow up and be asked to parties and dances if you don't learn how to be a lady? Saying 'ain't'! You can't be a tomboy all your life. You're seven years old. It's time for you to grow up."

"Does that mean I can wear lipstick, Mama?"

"What are you saying? Did I hear you right? My seven-year-old daughter, a little girl who shouldn't be thinking about things like that, asking her own mama if she can wear lipstick? God would punish me if I ever allowed such a thing." Her voice rising.

"I didn't mean anything, Mama. I don't even want to wear lipstick. I'm too little. I don't want to grow up. I don't want to be a woman."

Mama's face grows hard. I have made a mistake. I have used the 'woman' word.

"Women are colored and ladies are white."

It is the mantra of my childhood. My mama is white, my daddy is white, and I am white which means I must grow up to become a lady and mind my language, not stare, keep my legs together, wear dresses to church, and white gloves when I go shopping in New Orleans. There is a lengthy list of ladylike rules to follow. I dread growing up almost worse than I fear my mother's anger.

Mama thought being a woman was a wicked, forbidden thing. Even before I knew the word sex, I knew there was this thing inside of me that Mama wanted to root out and smash. She watched me for any transgression. She didn't care if I stole spending money out of her silver teapot, or if I scratched Brother's face till it bled, or if I made poor grades at school, or made the nuns angry.

I could eat in bed, miss school, ride my bike like a mad person, sit in the one-armed man's coke and ice cream store and read comics with the boys all morning on Saturdays. But I could not touch myself down there, a place that had no name other than dirty.

Even as a little girl, I suspected the forbidden place connected my secret longing to become a woman rather than the lady my mother wanted me to become, which, even as I write these words, forms part of my lifelong fascination with Ruby. I wanted to be a whole person not bound by what, even in childhood, seemed silly and false.

Ruby didn't seem to need to please Mama. She lived her life without fear of what the rest of the world thought, and she certainly never entertained the ambition of being something she wasn't.

Mama liked Ruby just fine the way she was. But her liking was more than about Ruby's skill with an iron. Ruby was a woman. I knew not because she was colored, but because she was true to herself. That would become my lifelong ambition, though I didn't know it yet. It would take me a good part of a lifetime to realize that even a lady could be wanton and like to feel what was down there in that special place.

In preparing for my first confession, which would happen right after Easter, I knew there was a list of sins I didn't even know the meaning of yet. I knew they were out there waiting for me. I knew my mama knew some terrible secret about me I didn't know yet. And whatever the secret was, it had something to do with my mother's fear I had too much woman in me to ever grow up and become a lady.

CHAPTER 3
The Chicken Coop

[1944]

During the years we lived on Military Road, Mama carried a deep sadness. She had married a man who didn't know how to love her, or be a real husband, or at least meet her expectation of what a husband should be.

Childhood memories of my father are fragmented. The strongest are sensory associations, such as the sour smell of beer, as he made the rounds of his favorite bars with me in tow. I still remember the feel of his arms encircling my thin body as he held me while we danced to the music of jukeboxes, and his scratchy beard rubbing against my face. In the drug stores where he worked as a pharmacist, my memory still holds the aromas of cod-liver oil mixed with the sweetness of Evening in Paris in its beautiful blue bottles, wrapped around the smell of malt and chocolate syrup and ice cream and the saltiness of frying hamburgers.

Sometimes memories come in a rush of images. On a cold windy day standing in front of Herbert's Drug Store where he worked, my father took my picture with a camera whose lens folded out from an accordion shaped box as I sat in the basket of our neighbor's bicycle, wearing my green corduroy jacket with a blue bandana on my head.

Soon after, he left to go off to WWII wearing a Navy sailor suit. I missed him and dreamed of his return when we would all live together and be happy ever after. He sent me a birthday card with a bear holding a large number three. It fit on my head like a crown and whispered that I was my daddy's princess.

My father was a man's man. A natural athlete, he'd played baseball in college. After the War, when he was too old to play on a regional team, he umpired minor league games he forced my brother and I to endure in the scorching, sun which often resulted in terrible sunburns. He also had a silly nickname, Chicken, which seemed to have more to do with his scrawny looks and angry disposition than his courage.

A sporty dresser, he wore golfing pants that caught his socks in the bands around the lower legs, making him look neat in wool argyle patterned socks and loafers. He wore white shirts under his sleeveless sweaters and bow ties on his skinny neck. He could never hold a job for long at the three drug stores in Covington because he was always slipping away to find a golf game or to Mr. Tugy's Bar at the Southern Hotel.

He raised cocker spaniels, so with each new litter, he loaded the puppies into cardboard boxes and took them to the blacksmith down by the railroad tracks. I was always his tag along.

I remember the sound of the hand-operated flint and the cry of puppies as their tails got cut off and cauterized. The smell of burning hair and flesh hung in the air and in my memory. I hid out inside the office while the cutting took place and gazed at the scantily dressed models on monthly calendars. But nothing could tune out the sound of puppies yelping frantically.

My father was also a fisherman and a hunter, and kept his guns in the deep, sloped ceiling closet under the staircase of our house. He kept his pistols wrapped in oil cloths and stuffed inside canvas bags. And the rifles propped up against slanting walls.

Fishing poles lay in a jumble on the floor with the ammo and tackle boxes side by side.

There were no locks on the gun closet. And after he left us, I would crawl into the forbidden darkness of that narrow space whenever I wanted to feel close to him. Sometimes, I hid inside the closet to get away from windows, but mostly I just wanted to be near the smells of my daddy. The smell meant he still belonged to our house and to me.

The large gas space heater, whose warmth rose following the stairwell to our attic bedroom, was on the outer wall of the closet. I think of it now and wonder if my parents worried about the proximity of so many explosive elements in our home. I remember Mama forbidding me to go into the closet, but, like so many children, danger did not seem to matter to me. It was the given. I was a little girl who wanted to be close to my daddy. And in that closet, I found at least a part of him. I found another part of him at the bars he took me to on weekends.

At Tugy's Bar, I am seven years old, still dancing on the bar as if I am three or four years old and my daddy had just come home from the War. The music is playing and I'm dancing for the joy of it and the men are all laughing. Some even offer me nickels and dimes.

My daddy is so drunk he thinks I'm cute. He not only allows me to dance; he encourages me to twirl my skirt. I'm wearing my pretty peach Sunday dress with the small pleats sewed into the bodice with red threads. The sash and skirt flare out, exposing my panties. I love the sound of the approving applause and the shouts of the men as they see beneath my dress.

Then, Mr. Tugy reaches up and takes me into his arms. He tells me it's not nice to dance on bars, and hands me over to my daddy.

"Don't bring this child here anymore, Chicken. What are you thinking, man?"

There is sudden silence. The men wait to see how my daddy is going to react. His face is red now and I'm tearing up and feeling ashamed. Something I had always done was suddenly inappropriate. Why didn't I know? Daddy puts his money on the bar and takes me by the hand as I follow him outside. He never speaks of it. I never forget.

It was during this time that my father gave Julian and me a quarter for the movies every Friday and Saturday night.

After the discovery of the Jewish Concentration camps and seeing the images of men at the wire fences surrounding the camps, I remember feeling I had to look, to see real people with eyes sunken from starvation. Some were naked, their bodies exposed to the cameras. But in school, I was hearing over and over that the Jews killed Christ. I couldn't reconcile any of it and no one wanted to talk about it.

Then there was the dropping of the atomic bombs on Hiroshima and Nagasaki. It would take years before I learned the full extent of the damage to its people and cities. Not to mention photos of the shadow images cast onto the walls.

Gradually, the images and the stories helped those of us who were young enough or open-minded enough to learn from the massive persecutions of innocent people. All that is necessary to result in a widespread change of heart.

Meanwhile, peace movements and the new vision of peace on earth preached by Martin Luther King would set off all the voices and movements that came later, but still in time for me to suffer the consequences of disapproval and rejection.

CHAPTER 4

Caregivers

[1944]

On weekends and summer mornings, I brought Mama her coffee and would crawl up next to her in bed while she drank the warm, bittersweet, chicory flavored mixture with boiled milk and sugar.

Her long, thick, dark hair wrapped around her face as she counted out her allotment of eight cigarettes. She lined them in a flat glass cigarette dish on the marble-top table next to the bed. The allotment of cigarettes, a compromise with the doctor, who told her she had to quit.

She smoked the first one of the day with me sitting in bed next to her, while she slapped at me as I tried to catch her exhaled smoke with my tongue but that was because Mama had tuberculosis and was afraid of her own germs

"Don't do that. I don't want to breathe on you. We must be extra careful. And don't let Ruby steal my cigarette butts, either."

Ruby loved tobacco more than Mama. Whenever she was at our house, she scraped the left behind tobacco off Mama's dirty ashtrays. She would tear off the cigarette paper smudged with my mother's lipstick and roll the shredded tobacco between her calloused thumb and index finger. When it was a compact ball, she pressed it into the crease between her lower gum and cheek. The brown juices dribbled out of her mouth in a thin stream, mixing with the black, snuff spittle already collecting at the corner of her dark and cracked lips.

"Ruby, Mama doesn't want you doing that. She's afraid of the germs."

"You just mind your business."

"But my mama said for me to tell you not to."

"It's my business. Don't you go telling her nothing about me."

Ruby and our maid, Betty, took turns keeping things going during the months when Mama had to spend her days resting. No one dared utter the word tuberculosis because it was nobody's business and Mama was afraid the Public Health people would make her go to a sanitarium like they did to her mother.

I don't believe Mama was afraid of dying as much as she was of being forced to abandon her children and her home. She was only thirty-one-years old in 1948, when she had baby Clay. And of course, she had us, me, age seven, and Brother, who was ten.

Our baby brother arrived in January of that year. He was a beautiful baby boy with dark eyes, long lashes, and a curly head of dark hair. When Brother and I could enter Mama and Daddy's bedroom, we found him wrapped in a soft, flannel blanket lying on our grandmother's old, green ribbon sofa that sat against the wall next to Mama's bed.

His small size surprised me. His tiny feet and hands were the size of my dolls. I thought he would arrive like a toddler.

They named him Clay Riggs after Mama's favorite uncle, Clay. I must not have heard that part because for a long time, most of my life, I believed he was named after the cliff of grey clay that looked over our river.

As much as Julian and I fought, we united in our affection for baby Clay. We changed his diapers and held bottles for him when Mama was too weak to nurse him. We were proud of our parenting skills. And for a while anyway, while mama was sick, he was ours.

We could not kiss Mama because of her illness, but when she was strong enough, she nursed. I loved to watch the hungry way Clay suckled our mother's breast and the way the milk collected on his cheek and mouth when he nuzzled her. Because of the holy cards the nuns at my school passed out for good behavior, I developed a mental picture of Mary nursing Baby Jesus, just the way Mama nursed baby Clay.

When I knew Mama was better, sat on the floor Indian style while she put on her make-up to go out into the world beyond our house. She had crooked teeth and didn't like to show them when she smiled, so there was a certain naturalness that was lacking in public. But in private, at least to me, she was the most beautiful woman in the world.

Not wanting to get lipstick on her teeth, Mama would use her finger to spread color onto her lips before rubbing them together and smiling into the mirror. Next she would spit on her mascara brush before dipping it into its container and then gently brushing the dark color onto her lashes.

Her eyes were grey like the cliff that hung over our river, and the contrast of the mascara gave them light. As she dusted her face with powder and gently applied her rouge, she would look down at me and caution, "It will be years before you are ready for make-up, but remember, just a little is better than too much. Too much and you cover up your natural beauty."

. . .

LIKE A FISH DENIED A RIVER

When we had visitors, Mama stepped into the bedroom when the time came to nurse our baby. I didn't understand. Why couldn't she nurse Clay in front of other people? They were friends, mostly other women. But she made one of her indisputable statements:

"Only colored women nurse babies in public."

The indisputable statements made Mama's face look hard and strained, but her expression was always beautiful while she looked down at our new baby.

It might seem strange, living on a river and all, but I suffered terribly from boredom.

Every afternoon after Clay was born, either Ruby or Betty waited for Julian and me when we got off the school bus. Mama had to sleep, and we had to be quiet and not wake her. If Clay was awake, we would play with him or put him in his bassinet near us.

Years later, when Clay was in his sixties, he almost died in a hospital in Boise, Idaho. I remember arriving during the day at noon and that when Julian arrived, he told the doctors and nurses how we took care of our little brother from birth.

"He's still our baby brother!" Julian had said.

It took three long weeks for Clay to fully recovery but none of us could leave Clay's bedside unless the other was there to stand watch.

Our maid, Betty's husband, Frank, was a minister in one of the churches in an area called Colored Town.

He was a large man with skin the amber color of our river. Frank moved slowly as he tended shrubbery and flowerbeds, raked pine needles, and gathered fallen branches. He was Mama's helper in the making of her garden.

I liked him because he didn't talk about sin. When he was around, I followed along listening to his soft, rich voice as he made his rounds in our yard. He taught me about a sweet Jesus and making do with what was at hand, which were the things I really needed to know.

Betty cleaned the house for us. Since we lived on a river, sand was a constant problem. Her skin was the color of Mama's morning coffee. Betty was thin and her movements were quick as she went from mopping to dusting, and from chore to chore.

For a year or more, Betty ruled the house. She was stricter than Ruby about doing homework and our being quiet. But she was able and willing to help me with my homework and would read aloud to me. Even though I was an excellent reader, I loved the sound of her rich voice.

Unlike Ruby, Betty didn't approve of tobacco. She didn't drink, cuss, or tell tales about the other white people she worked for. I know because Mama told me.

Betty spoke well, dressed neatly and properly in a grey uniform with white trim that was always clean, starched and ironed. She wore sturdy, nun shoes that were tied and had a slight heel. Her sharp tongue belied her generous nature.

"Miss Jere, uncross your legs. It doesn't look nice, and you'll get ugly veins when you grow old."

"Miss Jere, you go change out of that school uniform and don't let me see the skirt hanging on the bedpost."

"Miss Jere, you watch out for your baby brother... now don't go letting his head hang that way. You need to support his neck and head. That's right. You're going to make a good mama someday. You always love up on something. What fairy tale book do you want me to read from today?"

"The Red Shoes please, if there's time."

I loved orphan stories, and all the stories of children in trouble, because no matter what, the children always went to heaven.

LIKE A FISH DENIED A RIVER

Of course, you had to be dying and I happened to be aware of the many ways for a child to die.

The baby sister of a classmate died of pneumonia, and a classmate, a little boy who lived on a farm, stepped on a nail over summer vacation and died of lockjaw. I was sure that those children went straight to heaven.

And while I was afraid of hell, the nuns made sure of that, I wasn't afraid of dying during those years because I went to confession every week.

I just did not want my mother to die. There was no back-up for Mama. I needed her and was terrified of living without her.

Without knowing what it meant, I became hyper-vigilant about my mother's health. I knew I needed to live to take care of her and make sure she didn't die and leave my brothers and me orphans.

As much as I needed Betty to put order into my life and read the rich stories of hope and magic to me, it was the midnight black figure of Ruby who filled my thoughts.

Ruby with her strong stature and carriage, and the slimy black spittle that seemed to carry with it her many secrets hijacked my imagination.

She lived in a shack in the woods. I never saw it, Mama did. Everybody in town said Ruby was crazy and wondered why my mama put up with her. Mama just said, "Ruby is the best ironing woman anywhere and leave it alone."

But I knew Ruby was much more than our ironing woman. She did lots of things for us. But her big job, her real job, was to keep watch over us when we were alone.

Ruby kept a knife strapped to her thigh with an old belt. I know because I used to spy on her when she used the bathroom out in the garage.

I spied because I was curious about people of color. I was trying to figure out how they differed from white people.

But if I'm being completely honest, I spied on everyone.

I went through drawers and closets, not just at home, but in the houses of friends and relatives. I wanted to know why our family was as special as Mama kept telling me we were. But all my snooping and looking just made me realize how special other families were.

Other people had pantries stocked with canned foods, freezers that stored meat, and linen closets filled with towels that didn't have rough, torn edges. Some even had extra toothbrushes, and plenty of blankets and boxes of Kleenex.

Other girls had more than two Sunday dresses and their uniforms for Catholic school were perfect, with blouses that had all their buttons, blue oxfords and white socks that matched, and pajamas that fit.

They had lamps with working light bulbs next to their beds and didn't have to use flashlights or kerosene lanterns to read at night. They had sandwich meats and didn't have to eat mayonnaise or fried bacon grease sandwiches when they were hungry before bed. And they had more than two pots.

Before she went to bed on Sunday nights, Mama would cook starch in the same pot she used to cook custard ice cream on Sunday mornings.

When the starch was cool, she poured it into empty milk bottles and stored them on the top shelf of the refrigerator next to the milk. As her lungs caused her to grow weaker, I washed the pot before bedtime. And on cold, dry nights she made chocolate fudge from the Hersey box, stirring in peanut butter at the very end.

On Mondays, Mama washed clothes in our ringer washing machine and Ruby would emerge from the woods to help. With her skilled and strong hands, Ruby would shake out the clothes and linens that needed to be starched and after soaking them in the glutinous mixture would ring them out.

Then Ruby gave them a good shake and hung them to dry on the metal clotheslines that stretched between tall pine trees and the support beams of the old rose arbor.

Summer and winter, Ruby wore men's slippers on her big, calloused feet. The skin on her entire body was hard and cracked. She never looked put together. Nothing fit right and she limped because one hip was higher than the other.

She wore an old grey maid's dress that was ragged and held together with large safety pins. Someone or something had badly scarred her face. Her bloodshot eyes bulged, and she smelled like dead things, sweat and tobacco.

Ruby and Betty were early grounding posts for me. They not only put some order in the house, but they also witnessed what went on inside our family.

These two women of color, Ruby who was dark as night and Betty whose skin was like the color of rich milk chocolate, were my caretakers and guardian angels during the years of childhood when Daddy went crazy, and Mama couldn't deal with the terror of being left alone, particularly at night.

Mama would gather the four of us together to share the same room at night.

At first, it was a relief, at least for Julian and me, because there was no fighting when we were alone with our mother. But gradually, Mama's terror became our own.

CHAPTER 5

Easter Sunday

[1947 - 1948]

In a cycle that would go on for over a year, our father would move back in and then, after a fight, he would leave. Finally, he moved back home shortly after Clay was born.

I remember Brother and I ran down the stairs to find the dining room table covered with the green, cellophane grass that usually lined our Easter baskets. Hidden in the grass were small, yellow, fuzzy, artificial chicks, and spread out on the expanse of green were candy corn and jellybeans, gold brick candy bars and two large Gold Brick Eggs covered in foil and stuffed with individually wrapped nuggets of candy. There were also bowls of homemade fudge and hard-boiled eggs we dyed and decorated the afternoon before.

We couldn't taste any of it before church since we had to fast until after Mass. Even though I hadn't made my first communion yet, my mother decided I would join the fast early.

At church, Daddy, dressed in his suit and bow tie, was holding court at the table where the congregation paid their ten-cent pew rental fee. That ten cents were all some people could afford, and it went toward the cost of the Parish School, St. Peters.

After church, we rushed home to eat the eggs and divide up our candy. Later, there was a party and while the adults drank martinis, the children went to the Star Theater.

The movie that year was *Songs of the South*. I looked forward to it because it featured live actors and animation.

After the movie, happy and telling Mama about it, I sat on the stepstool between the stove and the icebox while she put away the bottles of starch she had cooked earlier. Daddy came in staggering drunk. He reached into the icebox to get out a bottle of milk. Before Mama could stop him, he tilted a full bottle of cooked starch into his mouth, then spit it out all over my pretty, new Easter dress. The bodice of it was covered in great globs of cold, congealed starch and spittle.

Then daddy pulled me so close to him I could feel his scratchy beard against my face as he looked at Mama and yelled, "Why do you have to put the starch in milk bottles? Look what you made me do!"

He started to brush the starch off my dress but I pushed him away, hating the smell of his breath and the feel of his scratchy beard.

I cried out, "You're drunk, Daddy!"

The sound of the slap was like a gunshot as he threw me to the floor.

Then Mama was screaming and Aunt Laura, my godmother, was there fussing at me. Her mouth was moving, and from her angry expression, I knew she was yelling. I had trouble hearing since the slap had landed on my ear and there was a ringing sound.

Finally, I heard, "Stop screaming, Jere. You're only making it worse. You're being dramatic."

I stuffed the dress into my mouth. But the sounds kept escaping. Then Daddy was choking Mama, shouting, and calling her names. I pushed on Daddy, and he let loose of Mama long enough to hit me again, and I flew toward the gun closet.

Then, Daddy had a gun, a pistol, pointed at Mama as he

threatened to shoot her. I walked toward him, staring at that gun the whole time, then slowly pushed it away as Daddy shouted at Mama that he was going to kill our baby.

Next, I remember I was in the bedroom with three-month-old Clay, picking him up and carrying him outside, past Brother who was sitting on a chest in the guest room, rocking back and forth, with a vacant look in his eyes. I knew he couldn't help.

I was afraid of the dark and the night, but it didn't make any difference. I sat in the dark shadows under a tall pine tree, rocking my baby brother and me, until Whoo Paw arrived to talk my daddy down.

Mama took the baby back into the house, and they sent me off to stay with friends where I turned down ice cream and cried those shuddering tears of a child who can't stop crying. When I finally stopped, I felt like I was drowning.

I have no memory of how we made the transition from that violent night. My face must have been bruised, so I would have been kept home from school until the bruises faded. The father of the family I stayed with was a doctor and I believe now he gave me medication to help me calm down.

My tears didn't drown me, but still I hadn't reached the surface from the deep hurt and terror of that Easter night.

When I finally went back home, both Daddy and Aunt Laura were gone. She had moved in with her youngest sister, Aunt Ellen, and her family.

At home it was only Mama, the baby, me, and Brother, who, during that time, busied himself building model planes. I wasn't allowed to touch any of his stuff, but he couldn't stop me from watching and breathing in the glue that came in tubes and had this distinctive odor that made us both feel better. And so it was that while engulfed in the odor of glue, I began a temporary healing from the events of Easter night.

The bottom drawer of the chest in Mama's room held treasure for me. And like my father's gun closet, it had its own distinct fragrances. Lingering smells of perfumes and old rosaries that had tarnished to gold after years of being fingered by praying fingertips and something else that would take me years to identify.

There were other keepsakes: old silver compacts and a hard, cardboard tube that held a tattered, large lady's fan with intricately carved, twelve-inch-long ivory ribs with rotting silk and tulle cloth sewn in. But the most important treasure was the scrapbook.

I sat on the floor in front of her dresser drawer, turning the familiar pages. Like Mama's eyes and the cliff that overlooked our river, the scrapbook was grey. Its pages filled with old newspaper articles and photos of Mama's cousin, a young doctor, lying on the marble floor of the Louisiana State Capitol. He was dressed in a white linen suit covered with dark patches of blood. Where his right eye was supposed to be was just a black hole. I would stare at that hole in his head with worry and question if it hurt?

The pages that followed held newspaper articles about his funeral and his medical studies at Tulane in New Orleans and Bellevue Hospital in New York, as well as his studies in Vienna and Paris. One of his high school teachers wrote a long testimony to his short but brilliant life.

The last pages held letters from Carl to my grandmother that began, "Dear Tante Tinnie."

I never met my cousin Carl Weiss. He died before I was born. According to my mother, Carl did not kill or in any way try to harm Huey Long.

"Nobody knows why he was in the Capitol that night." Mama's face would grow hard, as she envisioned her beloved cousin walking up those marble steps.

Even as a young child I knew my mother was trying to see what remained hidden in mystery. It was like when the nuns tried to get us to see inside our own minds the picture of Jesus dying on the cross, or becoming human again in the small communion wafer during the consecration of the Mass. Her dear dead cousin Carl was innocent, and that fact needed to be told over and over.

CHAPTER 6
The Power of Story

I learned to read in the one-armed man's soda fountain, comic-bookstore.

On Saturdays and summer weekdays, Mama or Daddy would drop Brother and me off in town to spend the day, or at least several hours on our own and away from them.

I always thought the one-armed man was a soldier who returned after the war. I asked him once how he lost his arm. "Was it in the war?" He snapped back it was none of my business. He handed me my coke with his hook hand and took the nickel I offered in the other.

"I lost my arm when I was a kid. I didn't get to kill any Japs or Nazis. Don't you go asking about where people lost their arm or anything else. Makes 'em feel bad."

He put his hook under the armpit of his good arm and looked at me.

"Now go read your comics." As I moved away, he called after me, "And how about buying one today?!"

There were two rooms on either side of the soda fountain room. Each side room had long wooden stands with three rows of comics. There were tables and chairs, but a lot of kids just sat on the floor in front of the racks, causing the searchers to climb over them. I don't remember a lot of girls.

I liked to sit on the floor, cross-legged and learned to read by associating words with the picture story lines in the adventures of Bugs Bunny, Mickey Mouse, and Donald Duck with his three nephews, Huey, Dewy, and Louie.

Later I would develop a taste for science fiction comics, longing for the day when I could travel through space or live in a futuristic city with elevated roadways that crisscrossed each other in spirals that seemed to reach for the sky.

At home, Brother had a set of Classic Comic Books, which were condensed stories with drawings and dialogue retold by writers like Mark Twain, the Bronte sisters, and Charles Dickens.

By the end of first grade, I had advanced to reading *Puddin' Head Wilson, Great Expectations, The Prince and the Pauper,* and *Wuthering Heights.* Sometimes the movie versions of these classic novels and stories would play at the Star Theater, or the nuns would show the movies on their noisy projector in the basement of St. Peter's School.

But the stories in those comics, read and reread, had more to do with my moral development than any catechism class or sermon, even more than my mama.

The customs and traditions that encased my childhood conflicted with the themes of justice in these stories that taught me to challenge accepted beliefs and codes of honor and manners. I developed an early hypercritical eye for injustice and a longing to write my impressions of the world.

And then, for Christmas, we received a set of fairy tales. The green book held the stories by Han's Christian Anderson, the red book held many of the Grimes Brothers Fairytales. They were difficult for me, but I could still read them. And I loved having Betty read them to me during the troubled time after Easter.

. . .

In 1948, Ottilie Lambert was the town librarian. She was a tall spinster woman with long hair held in place with braids looped over the top of her head like a crown.

Mama would have washed my mouth out for calling her a woman, but she seemed too real to be a lady. For me, she was an adult who did not lie.

The town library was in search of a home. For a while it was in a brick row of stores next to the one arm man's store. It finally found a standalone home in a small brick building across from the Post Office.

Once a month or so, Ottilie would hold Saturday library days for the town's children. One time, she brought in a Native American to teach basket weaving.

We had art days, and while we painted or used scissors to cut out snowflakes and flowers, she read to us from story books. She introduced us to the world of culture, to a world bigger than our small town or even New Orleans. Then one Saturday, Ottilie took me aside.

"Jere, I notice you never take library books home."

"No, Ma'am."

I didn't want to tell her I couldn't be sure I could return them on time. Our life was too chaotic to plan anything other than going to school. And things like library books could get lost.

"Don't you like to read? I see you reading comic books at the soda fountain."

"Yes Ma'am, I like to read."

"Do you read books at your home? Your mother is a great reader. Do you just read comics?"

"No Ma'am. I read fairy tales."

"Which are your favorites?"

"I like the *Red Shoes*, and the one about the Angel who takes the poor sick boy up to heaven, and *The Girl Who Trod on a Loaf*."

"Those were all written by Hans Christian Anderson. Do you know what they have in common?"

"The children all die and go to heaven?" I answered quickly without having to think about it.

Ottilie nodded her head.

"And there's a wonderful light at the end." I added and nearly shouted.

"There's a word for that light. 'Transformation.' The children are all transformed, changed."

"Like the little girl who walked on the bread changes into a bird?"

"Yes. Like that. Do you like the Brothers Grimm stories?"

"Un huh, *Cinderella*, and the *Twelve Princesses* who dance their shoes away, oh and *Snow White*..."

"What else? Do you like poetry?"

"I have a set of *Wonder Books*. I like to read the poems and nursery rhymes and stories when I'm sick or can't sleep."

"That's good, but I want you to read a book from here. You can tell me about it when I come to your mother's coffee week after next."

The ladies of Covington hosted small afternoon parties called coffees for the different holidays and seasons. Mama planned her gatherings during December.

I picked out a book, some child's book, in the section she directed me to. But I didn't like it. It was too much like my readers at school.

Instead, I began exploring Mama's shelves. Mama caught me looking at my favorite book cover. It had a picture of the windshield of an old truck that reminded me of my Smith grandfather's old black Ford. Hanging from the rearview mirror was a set of dice. Taking the book from my hands, she said, "You may read any book on these shelves except this one."

"Why, Mama?" I hadn't intended to read it. It was too thick a book for me. The title was strange. I had been reading it out loud to myself.

"*The Grapes of Wrath*. What does it mean, Mama?"

"Nothing. It was written by a communist. And the less said, the better. I'm just sorry I read it."

I knew it must be awfully bad because we prayed after mass every Sunday for the conversion of Russia and the fall of communism. Everybody knew the communists were all going to hell.

As always, Mama planted the seeds of rebellion in me. Reading it didn't really matter right then. I just liked the cover. But I vowed to read it someday.

I was actually looking for a very thin book. I only had a week before Ottilie came for Mama's Coffee and I'd made a promise I would read an entire book.

Searching the shelves I finally found, if not the thinnest book, one whose title I could understand. *'When the Mountain Fell'* was a short novel by C.F. Ramuz, first published in French in the 1930s under the title Deborence. The English translation on my mother's shelf had a 1946 publication date. Its cover was marked as a book of the month selection. It was a book Ottilie would have been familiar with.

It began with a quote, "A Shepard, missing, and presumed dead, spent several months buried in his cabin, living on bread and cheese..." Those opening words held my imagination captive.

I did not understand the short novel's underlying meaning was about the rise of fascism in Europe. And I did not know what an allegory was yet, but I knew about fairy tales and folk tales. And because of movies and comic books, I had a visual imagination and could easily envision the young Shepard struggling to survive while trapped in dark tunnels under the mountain of snow that buried him.

I marveled at how he captured melting snow that found its way into where he crawled. And how he ate the food in his pocket and the food he found in the pockets of his dead companions.

I could understand that he talked to a dead man who did not answer just to hear a human voice, even his own. As young as I was, I could relate to that same longing.

. . .

The day of Mama's Coffee I handed the book to Ottilie.

"This is the book you read, child? Jere, could you understand the book at all? This is an adult book. Tell me what you read."

"A big piece of the ice and lots of snow fell off a mountain and buried some men. They were sleeping. Everyone thought they were dead, but one lived in the dark for a long time. He had to melt snow to drink and had a little bread of his own and he had to steal bread from the dead men, and he had to climb through rocks, but finally he made it above ground. His head came up to the sunlight and he couldn't see. Everyone thought he was a ghost. Sad, he went back to the mountain. But his wife saved him and brought him home." I took a deep breath before finishing. "And the sun was shining."

Ottilie smiled.

"I see. It's like a fairy tale, isn't it? Which one? Hans Christian Anderson or the Grimm's Brothers?"

I smiled, "Hans Christian Anderson!"

"When you grow up, I want you to read it again. I think you're almost ready to read longer stories and books by great writers. We'll start with the stories of Mark Twain and maybe...we'll see." She called to my mother, "Winnie, this girl's going to be a writer."

"Julian's my writer, Ottilie."

"You'll see Winnie; this girl is going to write stories."

CHAPTER 7

The Powers that Be (Part 1)

*"How should we know the
things which we believe?"*

*"We shall know the things we believe
from the Catholic Church;
through which God speaks to us."*

Baltimore Catechism, Blue Book

[1948]

I never spoke in third grade. I was tongue tied, and miserable because my uniform was discombobulated and I feared Sr. Agatha might ask about the safety pins that replaced missing buttons, or the flapping soles on my saddle oxfords, or why my hair stuck up every which way? And also that she might ask about the bow tie I could never get right, in part because Mama refused to buy me shirts with Peter Pan collars.

Sr. Agatha who taught third and fourth grades never mentioned those failings. Instead she opted to torture me with the catechism and my name.

I had been named after my mother and grandmother, Winifred, but I was nicknamed Jere. Every day Sr. Agatha's ritual was to call me me to my feet and the sound of Winifred or Winnie was foreign to my ear.

The only thing worse than third grade was the knowledge that even if I passed to fourth grade, I would remain in the class of the meanest nun ever.

Sr. Agatha had a sister named Anna, who was also a nun.

Sr. Anna taught me in second grade and prepared me for my first communion. She was as sweet and beautiful and petite as her sister was angry, awkward, and tall.

Years later, I discovered both sisters were orphans raised by the Benedictine Order, who had early on decided that Anna and Agatha would become teaching nuns. It was a matter of economics.

The teaching Orders needed lots of women who would teach without demanding salaries, and the women needed a place to live and food to eat. So, like marriages based on dependency, it led to a hopelessness expressed in anger and cruelty, or in a passively layered protective coating of sweetness.

St. Peter's was the Parish school for St. Peter's Catholic Church.

A long, wide hall divided the classrooms from front to back and ended in an area designated as the library. In the middle of the hallway, a doorway led into a cloakroom and a storage room that held a closet for placing bad little children.

Their screams would ring through the entire school, filling the listening children's ears and hearts with terror, or memories of their own time spent in the locked closet.

There were other sounds too. The sound of spankings, and of leather straps hitting skin as the children's pleas for mercy resounded beyond the halls and deep into all of our memories.

. . .

My first day in her class, Sr. Agatha, loomed over me.

Her habit comprised a long black dress covered with a long slip over a bib-like garment; the layers held in place by a leather belt. And looped over the belt was a large set of rosary beads with a crucifix hanging at one end. The sturdy laced shoes she wore and the cotton stocking that covered her legs were black. Under the long veil, which was also black, and reached down to her fingertips was her wimple, or white head and neckband with a pleated collar. The wimple held her face tightly, causing her flesh to bulge. The skin on her face was red and chaffed from the constrictive head covering, making her look even more menacing.

"Winifred, do they call you Winnie?"

"My mother's called Winnie. My name is Jere, Sister."

"Jere is not a saint's name. Winifred was a saint. Who made the world, Winnie?

"That was my baptismal name. My name is Jere, Sister."

She holds a wide menacing ruler in her right hand. My eyes do not leave it.

"Come here, Jere, and hold out your hand."

My feet refused to step forward. I stood at my desk, unable to move. I had never been hit at school.

"Come here, Jere."

She held her ruler up high like a wand.

"This is for impertinence and inappropriate behavior. Do not cry."

She knew the tears were coming. I swallowed deep inside myself the lump that had grown huge inside my throat. I went to the front of the room and faced the class as she slapped my hands three times. I did not cry as I gave her my left hand. I brought my hand back up to the proper level after each strike. My hand burned like fire.

"Now the right hand."

She took my right hand in hers and lifted it. I had broken

both my arm and wrist the previous spring and was protective of it. I struggled not to pull away, terrified it would break again.

"This is for talking back to your teacher."

The lump grew bigger.

"Now go back to your seat."

I told my mother. I was never hit again, but the damage was done.

My ability and desire to please my teacher was replaced by a desire to disappear. I was driven by the sure knowledge I was in a life and death struggle at home and at school.

"Winnie, stand."

Then the question.

"*Where is God?*"

I stood mute, my mind blank. I knew the answer was somewhere in my head, but I had lost the connection to retrieve, to breathe, to function. My lips could not form words.

"Well, try this one. *Does God know all things?*"

Silence. Every day, except for the days I was sick, the repetitive questions followed by my silence.

Illness was a blessing that year. Ear infections were the plague of my childhood, but in third grade, an earache was a cheap price to pay to stay home, away from Sr. Agatha.

Each afternoon, I'm sent home to write out the missed questions three times.

Math was a challenge, but Sr. Agatha spent no time worrying herself or me over division or fractions. She made sure I would become a theologian, able to pull up those foundation questions and answers from somewhere deep in my brain.

I didn't just memorize them. I learned them. I argued with them, took them to church with me, when I would pay the recommended weekly private visit there. I knelt, not at the statue of Mary, but at the foot of the large crucifix that hung near the altar rail.

My prayers came in the form of questions.

"Is it true? Can God see me all the time?"

"Do you know what I'm really thinking right now?"

"If my soul is more important than my body, where is my soul?"

"Will I go to hell if I go into the Baptist church?"

"Do you really only love Catholics?"

Like the mystics, I would stare at the figure on the cross, Jesus' body hanging, naked except for a loin cloth. In changing baby Clay's diaper, I had become more familiar with the male physiology than my own.

"Do you have a *Peter pot*?" I held my breath.

"Oh, Lord, I am heartily sorry. Did that make you mad?"

"Is it a sin to talk to you?"

"I love you Jesus."

"Thank you for making me white. Why didn't you just make everybody white?"

In the late fall, Sr. Agatha chose me to represent our class by delivering a narrative poem at the Christmas pageant.

It was a long poem, three pages. It had to be memorized. I was afraid I might not remember or be too afraid to speak, but I loved the poem. It was a sad story about a sick child who died, and a little girl made well again who got a bicycle.

I identified with that little girl because I wanted a bicycle for Christmas. I memorized the poem by writing it over and over, learning it section by section.

Our maid, Betty, helped me. Mama had the seamstress make me a beautiful green dress with a huge sash, and I wore a white lace covering called a dickey over the bodice.

. . .

On the night of the Christmas Pageant, I walked on stage and looked out at the audience. Sr. Agatha had cautioned me to keep my eyes looking straight out over the heads of people. But I looked. I looked directly at the audience and I loved what I saw.

The basement where we played on rainy and frigid days filled with wooden folding chairs and every one of them held a parent or sibling or a family friend.

I was home. It was like dancing on Mr. Tugy's bar, only better because it was a stage. My voice came out loud and clear and I never missed a word. I didn't even worry or think about not remembering. The words flowed out of me.

My mama was near the front next to Brother. Baby Clay was home with Betty. I would tell her all about it when we got home.

On the way out of the auditorium, Sr. Agatha said, "I knew you could do it." That's all she ever said.

I continued my silence in class. As the winter turned into spring, she developed a new way to torture one of the country boys. A sweet boy who never missed class, whose mother must have cut his hair with a bowl on his head and shaved from his neck up to the edge of the bowl.

One day Sr. Agatha held a jar up for the class to see.

"This is a tapeworm. You get them from going barefoot around a barn where animals live."

Then she had the sweet boy stand in front of the class and told us he had tape worms.

She asked him whether he wore shoes around the barn. Every student who understood the poverty that surrounded us knew children who lived on the small farms saved their only shoes for school and church. And without fully understanding it, I now had a marker for how prejudice manifests in casual society.

The fights between Brother and me grew increasingly violent and constant, often ending with me scratching his face. He would act superior and play tricks designed to make me feel stupid.

One time, it got so bad, Daddy bought us a set of boxing gloves for Christmas. They were red, or maybe that was my blood.

Our father stood us in the living room and coached me to keep my guard up and how to keep moving. Brother was a head taller than me. What was our father, thinking?

As soon as he stepped back, Brother's long right arm came out swinging and smashed me in the face before I could think to protect myself. I don't know which pain I hated worse: being hit in the nose by my brother or slapped across the face by any adult who felt I needed a lesson in respect.

Our father remained in our lives, coming and going, in and out, living at home, taking jobs in other small towns, or living in the Southern Hotel when he came to see us.

And I had to honor him with my love, even when he was drunk and mean. It was the Fourth Commandment. No wonder I stopped praying to God, a father I could not even imagine. And finally, sometime in 1949, when I was in third grade, it all came crashing down.

Mama and Daddy have been fighting. He's drunk. There is a bad storm raging outside. Mama packs my brothers and me into the car and drives us through the rain. I don't know where we're going. The rain is beating against the windshield, and she is crying and having trouble seeing as she recites a prayer to the Blessed Mother. Brother and I are quiet. Clay sits between us, or we take turns holding him.

"Mary Mother of God, never was it known that anyone who implored your help..."

There is a siren and flashing lights behind us. It is lightening and thundering. Mama cries harder because she doesn't know what to do. She is afraid.

The Sheriff comes up to the driver's side. He is dressed in a yellow slicker and hat with a flap that covers his neck and has a beak covering his sheriff cap. Water pours off him.

"I'm sorry Miss Winnie, but you got to go back home. Chicken called in a stolen car report."

"This is my car, too."

"Sorry Mis' Winnie, the car's registered in Chicken's name. It doesn't belong to you. You know that."

"But he's drunk. I need to take my children to a safe place. I'm going to my Daddy."

"Can't be helped, the law says I must make you go back home and return the car to its rightful owner. Or put you in jail. Now, nobody wants that. I'll make sure he leaves and spends the night in town."

"You're just a bastard, like the rest of them!"

"Come on, Miss Winnie, don't be giving me any trouble. Just think of these kids."

Shortly after our father left us for good, strange things happened.

The phone line would suddenly go dead. This was especially frightening to my mother because much of the time, she didn't have a car.

Like most families, we only had one car, a taupe-colored Studebaker. Daddy loved Studebakers with their clean lines and sporty front seats. When he moved out, he took the only car with him.

Occasionally he would let Mama use it, but usually she had to make do without. Since the house was several miles from the town and no neighbors were close enough to hear her screams for help, the phone was her lifeline to the world. The car became a control stick for our father.

The sheriff thought an animal was causing the problems with our phone line. The telephone man said otherwise. He found signs someone had crawled under the house to where, beneath my mother's bedroom, the phone line was stapled to one of the cross beams supporting the floorboards and pulled them out. With each outage, the phone man would return. I remember him holding up the frayed wires for my mother to see.

"Mrs. Smith, no animal did this. These wires weren't cut. Look, you see the ends are frayed. Somebody with superhuman strength tore these wires apart. I'd be careful if I was you."

If he meant to scare her more than she already was, he succeeded.

We all became increasingly terrified. On the long nights when Mama was alone with just us children, she gave in to a Southern lady's greatest fear.

The nightly visitor was a peeping Tom. A Negro man with super powerful strength who had heard she was now a lone woman without a man to protect her. Mama began to keep a pistol by her bedside. She didn't know how to load the thing, but it gave her a sense of power.

Aunt Ellen and Uncle L.C. were living in New Orleans and while they could come on weekends, the prowler never appeared when others were there.

They let their golden cocker, Mickey, stay with us to serve as a watchdog. Mama kept him by her bedside to warn her of the stranger's approach.

She also moved Brother and me into her bedroom. I slept with her and Brother on Nanee's old sofa pulled next to the bed while baby Clay still slept in his crib.

The garden my mother planted so lovingly became overrun with water moccasins attracted to its cool shade and pockets of water, and they sometimes left their shade to crawl through the yard.

To save my life and make it so I was not afraid to ever leave the house, Mama had to teach me the difference between good snakes that were nonpoisonous, and bad snakes that could kill me. So, she had Brother, who was allowed to be unafraid of anything, catch and bring up to the house specimens of the different good snakes that were common to our yard and the woods beyond.

There were green snakes, deep brown ground snakes, ribbon snakes and the beautiful, multicolored king snakes that grew huge and looked dangerous, but weren't. Brother held out a king snake for me to touch.

"Here, feel it."

Terrified to be so close to a snake, I cringed and hid my eyes.

"No, it's slimy."

"No, it isn't, stupid. It's dry and warm from the sun. Feel it."

"Don't call your sister *stupid*."

Try it, honey, he's right. Snakes aren't slimy, I promise. Good snakes aren't."

Mama took my hand in hers.

"Come on, we'll just touch the side of it together so you can feel it for yourself."

Brother inched the snake closer with its head pointing at me, causing me to scream and Mama to step in, "Julian, behave! Don't frighten her. She must learn. Just hold it out lengthwise."

Slowly, taking my hand in hers, my mother helped me lose my fear of snakes. Before the lesson was over, I could touch each snake's head and body. Mama and Brother were right. The snakes felt warm and dry to my touch.

Before the summer was over, I could pick up snakes from the grass, grabbing them close to their head, just in case, and I always made sure Brother was close by.

Mama let us keep a few of them. By day, they lived in cages. But at night, we let them out while Mama sat in her faded, green, damask chair next to the white, marble-top table with the lamp whose shade she had covered with the pinned butterflies she caught with Daddy's old fishing net.

One at a time, Brother and I put the snakes on the cool

marble and watched them curl around the lamp, seeking the warmth of the light bulb. While Mama sat holding our baby brother Clay, we allowed our strange pets to curl around our arms and legs as we listened to the music of Brahms on the old, portable record player.

Mama made frequent calls to the Sheriff who made her go back home that stormy night.

He would send deputies out with hound dogs, who would catch the sniff of someone under the house and head off toward the river, where the scent would soon dissipate.

However, the sheriff was no help on those long nights spent with a dead phone line. Finally, he decided to assign a lone deputy to spend the nights. The deputy would sit straight up in one of our dining room chairs, in the middle of the living room holding a shotgun across his legs.

He must have been the oldest deputy on the force because what was left of his hair was white. His body and face were emaciated, wrinkled and discolored with large red and blue spots common in older adults, or someone who spent a lifetime working in the sun.

If he slept, it was with his eyes open. Brother and I couldn't sleep after so many disruptions and we made a game of spying on the old man, trying to catch him snoring or showing some sign, he was falling asleep on the job.

Whoever was terrifying our mother was smart and careful. He stayed away if the deputy was on guard. But on the nights we were alone, he returned.

Mama would leave the dog outside on the advice of friends and the sheriff.

One night, we heard the dog barking and looked out the

upstairs window. By this time, we were sleeping upstairs, with the bedroom door bolted shut.

When we looked out the window we couldn't see anything, but the dog began to whimper as we heard something like a board or log hitting him. Brother and I grew hysterical, shouting out into the night, "Leave our dog alone!"

Mama had put Brother in charge of loading the gun as she yelled epitaphs out the window, so on another night when he handed her the gun, she shot right through the screen.

She emptied the gun as we listened, and waited to hear footsteps coming up the stairs. We sat huddled together until morning despite the heavy chest we had pushed up against the door to the stairs for extra protection.

It was never determined who frightened Mama and us children. Was it our father or some mysterious colored man? A young, country boy set on rape and terror, or plain meanness? Or maybe, even the sheriff?

It remains a mystery, something Julian and I speculate on from time to time, always in the end determining it was our father who, in one of his drunken paranoid destructive states, stalked us.

CHAPTER 8

The Powers that Be (Part 2)

D addy had it firm in his mind that baby Clay was not his child, and that Mama had had an affair.

Aunt Virginia, losing patience with our father's lack of responsibility, writes to the lawyers that Henry is not to be allowed to sign anything or use her name.

It was then that her husband and my godfather, Harry, drove from their home in Shreveport to make surprise visits. They wanted to make sure we were all safe.

Harry was a fine amateur photographer, and he chronicled the sadness and despair written over the faces of Brother and me. He also took the only formal photos of Mama and Clay.

He and Mama would sit and talk over cups of *café au lait* while I watched out for Clay, who was an active toddler by then.

Meanwhile, Mama and Virginia did not get along, yet Harry seemed like a savior to me during those brief visits. Sadly, he had to leave us for his own family, so he did not witness what was happening as our father stopped giving Mama any money.

It was during that summer when I was eight that I made a magical discovery.

If I pressed my body against a pillow and rode it like a horse, a sensation of soothing warmth would flood through me and make the part I was never to touch, wet, and the rest of me sweaty and liberated from the feeling of fear.

I was sure this feeling was mixed up with Jesus or God and that is was a gift offered from heaven to comfort me.

Early on, Mother caught me.

"Stop that. You might hurt yourself."

I was red-faced and embarrassed and not sure why.

"What were you thinking about just then?"

The question terrified me. What I was thinking about?

The experience seemed harmless up until that moment, when my mother made it forever forbidden and shameful.

Could Mama read my mind like the all-knowing God of the *Baltimore Catechism*?

What had brought me such pleasure now took an unpleasant turn. It wasn't the action, making my body sweaty. That part was still a gift from God. But could she read my thoughts?

A seed planted with deep roots, as all my thoughts became sinful. Childhood fantasies wrapped their arms around my psyche and would not let go.

For the remainder of my childhood and into adulthood, my fantasies were formed first about nuns and later when I reached puberty about being spanked by men.

I was both victim and abuser.

Buried memories of blackout curtains during WWII when our daddy was away on a ship in the Pacific, and when we stayed with our mother's parents and aunts in a crowded New Orleans apartment resurfaced.

They were memories mixed with scary movies and the sounds of cruelty, and the teachings about God knowing our thoughts as well as our actions. Memories of when I became terrified of windows because I knew deep down you couldn't really escape, and that there was danger on the outside just waiting.

In the attic bedroom where Brother and I slept, there were no curtains, so I hid my head under the covers to hide from the moon.

Even hiding did not help because in a dream I saw a green kite with a malevolent face looking down at me as I slept. The image crept into my head and the terror of it would not leave me.

I did not yet know the face was the face of the all-knowing, judging God fed into the minds of little children to make us afraid of our own bodies and thoughts.

All these terrifying thoughts and dreams happened during the same time Mama shot Daddy's old pistol into the night from an attic window and the phone went dead.

During the daytime, Ruby or Betty would be at our house when we got off our school bus.

By this time, Mama was extremely sick. She slept most of the day, and Julian and I stopped fighting and tried to help by obeying Ruby and Betty.

Mama wrote her sister and our favorite Aunt Billie to come help her. It took a while for Billie to finish up her job and leave her life in Atlanta where she still had a chance to find a nice man and have children of her own, but we all hoped in our hearts she would come.

In the meantime, someone else joined our afternoon caregivers.

An old French lady we called Miss Sasseneau who taught me to embroider cross stitches across the hems of our pillowcases. It gave me time to calm down and give my fears a rest.

I have no idea who paid anyone. Our cupboard was almost empty. And Mama's flesh was disappearing. Her breasts were flat with large nipples. Her clothes hung on her. When she wore her swimsuit to go down to the river, her bones were exposed.

. . .

One sunny day Aunt Billie arrived like a vision of hope with her new hair style, a short poodle cut and strawberry blonde hair.

We had no car, half a jar of peanut butter, jelly, bread and milk and eggs. But only because the milk man delivered them.

She took over the guest room and fixed her and Mama a bourbon with ice and water.

After taking a deep breath she said, "The only thing to do is to rent this house to a family from New Orleans for the summer and rent an apartment or small house in town."

And that is how I got to go to the Baptist Bible Camp during the summer between third and fourth grade. Mama's Catholic friends were scandalized, and her atheist friend told her in front of me that she was going to totally confuse me.

They were all wrong. It was the best summer ever. The camp was at the public school, and we had crafts, and treats, and sang our hearts out and nobody got hit or cried. On the last day, the minister of the Church came up and asked how the camp was for me.

"I loved it sir. The only thing I'm sorry for is, I can't pray with you."

"Jere darlin, you don't have to worry about praying. We just wanted you to have fun."

It was a fun summer. Julian and I still got to swim but in the big Bogue Falaya at the State Park. And when we walked to the movies, he'd run ahead and jump out to frighten me.

And Whoo Paw loaned us his old Packer. So, when the summer was over, Aunt Billie could get to her job and then Mama traded the house on Military Road to a lawyer from New Orleans and his wife, who spent their summers in Covington. Julian almost broke the deal, which was putting more cash into Mama's bank account than she thought possible.

The wife of the buyer told Mama in front of us she planned to get rid of the tropical plants in the gully because they attracted snakes and she was afraid of them. She didn't understand that the snakes were in the gully because it flooded, and the shade attracted the snake anyway, and the garden was Mama's making.

It was beautiful to look at. And not wanting to move anyway, Julian played one of his tricks on the buyer's wife.

He took one of his snake boxes out of the place where we kept them and was acting strange with it. The lovely lady got curious and called out, "Julian, what you got there?"

"Oh, nothing you would be interested in."

"Now you come over here and show me or I'll tell your mother."

"Okay, but I don't think you'll like it," he said, as he slowly opened the door at the top.

When she saw that snake, she started screaming and then couldn't catch her breath. For once Mama got mad at my big brother. And as soon as the older lady got her breath back she accused Julian of being a wicked boy.

It was true, of course, and he reveled in her reaction because he didn't really want to leave the river house.

When we finally moved, it was to the house on 19th Avenue during the early spring of 1951.

Mama gave me my own room which was already painted in my favorite color, and had yellow plaid wallpaper. My bed was the old three-quarter bed from the attic room on Military Road and Mama painted an old chest white. The room had French doors that opened to a screen porch where Mama and her friends would drink coffee and talk.

The previous owner had left café curtains on the windows and glass-framed doors.

I would crawl up behind the curtained doors to listen quietly to their talk.

. . .

One afternoon, mother was sitting with her artist friend, Miriam.

Mama had spread olive oil on her own legs and was shaving them. She wiped the dark, short stubbles that clung to the razor onto a towel. It must have been hot because Mama had on white shorts and Miriam was wearing a sundress. I heard Mama apologize.

"I know it's not ladylike to do this in front of you, but we're good enough friends."

Miriam didn't seem to care. She seemed intent on Mama's legs.

"Winnie, you should wax your legs. You wouldn't have to do that all the time."

"I tried waxing my eyebrows once. It hurt so much I thought my eyes were getting plucked out of their sockets."

"Winnie, you're exaggerating."

Mama eyed Miriam's legs.

"I have longer legs than you. And if I put wax on them there is no way to melt the wax off, so if I don't like it, I'm forced to keep pulling."

In a muffled voice, Miriam said, "You know some women wax other parts of their bodies." They both laugh.

I wanted to imitate the sounds of their laughter. It was a mysterious sound, low like a growl. But I stayed quiet so I could listen and smell their perfumes, Mama's favorite, *Toujours Moi*, and Miriam's mixed with their cigarettes, and their secret woman odors.

In Mama's contradictory teachings I learned ladies did not smell. It was her way of separating herself from colored women. As I secretly listened to their conversation and the sounds of their laughter, I knew no matter what she said, my mother was a woman, and I liked her better that way.

. . .

Before Mama got so sick, I remembered the smell of dirt mixed with sweat as she worked in the garden alongside Betty's husband, Frank. Her black hair would curl and get into her eyes. I watched as she wiped it out of the way and tied her hair back with an old bandana that grew stiff with sweat as it dried.

Mama would take a break and sit on the backsteps drinking a cup of coffee.

Those memories are all mixed up with memories of Frank, as he showed me how to rake pine straw up into lines that became the blueprint for the rooms of make-believe houses.

In that long, deep yard that ran between our house and the bamboo hedge, I whiled away the sizzling summer afternoons designing and building my future homes. I moved from room to room, naming each and imagining what my houses would look like when I grew up and had babies of my own. But that was before tuberculosis.

During the summer of 1950, horses became my passion. At a nearby stable, I learn to ride and saddle a horse in exchange for minor chores, like brushing horses and filling their feedbags and raking around the stalls.

The stable was owned or at least run by a Black man named Joseph. He was a huge man and wore cowboy boots.

By that time, I was nine years old and still small enough to be afraid of the size and snorts of the horses. But I was determined to learn to ride and not be so afraid.

I remember my first day in the saddle and the feel of my secret place pressing against it while feeling the horse's every movement. The sensation felt similar to when I was riding my pillow pressed between my legs, but even then, I realized it was different because my gift was a secret connection to my body. And being in the saddle was not a secret connection but rather vital to keeping me balanced and aware of what the horse might be thinking.

· · ·

I knew Mama didn't like me spending so much time at the stables and sometime in late summer she told me Joseph had come to the house and told her my daddy had said he could have one of his old fishing poles in the garage.

Sure, he was lying, she told me I couldn't go to the stable anymore because Joseph was 'uppity.' When I tried to disobey her Joseph told me I couldn't come anymore and to not make trouble for him.

I remember running, trying to hide myself in the woods nearby. Joseph telling me I couldn't come to the stable anymore felt like the burn of Ruby's iron, and the sting of Betty's slap against my face all at once.

I'd broken a rule I didn't fully understand. Joseph had trusted me to do simple things around the stable and as I lost my fear of the horses, I could mount and ride those behemoth beasts.

The week before I was forbidden to go to the stable, Joseph had been on a ride with a group of teenagers. They passed our new house and seeing me and my aunt, invited me to ride with them, and Aunt Billie said it would be okay.

Joseph reached down his arm, and I hooked on as he swung me up and back behind him. I held on until I balanced myself.

Mama must have seen this as a dangerous breach of all that is holy. Later in the ride down a two-lane highway, a speeding car caused our horse to rear and slide down a long grade that kept the road high and dry. I held on to Joseph for dear life as he and the horse ended up with me under them.

After what seemed a long time, the horse found his feet. Frank, who had a scared look on his face, found me buried in the dry leaves and soft mulch. I scrambled to my feet, and declared, "I'm fine."

The teenagers who rode down the steep grade to make sure we were okay all clapped.

The only lie was about the fishing pole. I don't know if Mama and Joseph ever had a talk. But a clear boundary had been crossed for each of them.

And since neither my mother nor Joseph had the words or inclination to explain the why of it, I was left to take blame for the loss of trust I had gained in myself that last summer. Like most children who accept the burden of blame, I eventually found a way to begin again and to trust once more.

The previous owners had converted the old wooden garage behind our new house into a horse stable. Their only child, a daughter, was an accomplished rider.

The parents attached a corral to the stable by fencing in a grassy area at the back of the property. I knew we couldn't afford a horse, but even sitting in the empty stable brought me contentment as I inhaled the lingering odors of horse, feed, and manure.

I now think my attraction to dark spaces was like my grandfather's hardware store, daddy's gun closet and Mama's bottom drawer; the barn was private and had strong odors that somehow connected me to myself. And that connection made me feel safe.

Mama planted green beans and tomato vines to cover the chain-link fence at our new home.

She placed raw liver around the stable to attract fleas that infested the barn and its surroundings; and when those fleas gathered for the banquet, she covered them with lye. I would watch fascinated as the pests died a horrible death. Yet sitting there observing the dying fleas amidst the shadows in the barn, I felt safe.

Then the young man who helped my daddy when we still lived on Military Road, by doing odd jobs, came into the barn one summer afternoon. Mama hired him to do odd jobs for her.

He stood behind me and, through my blue jeans, rubbed the forbidden area between my legs. "See how good that feels?"

It felt funny, like a tickle, almost good. Then something I almost forgot resurfaced about another time when we still lived on Military Road and he did that same thing.

It also reminded me of dancing with my daddy, and how I was confused and had to fight my way out of his arms. But it didn't remind me of riding a horse or rubbing myself against my pillow.

I may not have had a word for it yet, but it felt nasty.

"Don't you go telling your Mama. She's not going to do anything, and you'll get in trouble."

I was going to be in trouble, no matter what. So, I ran into the house, and I told Mama.

I never saw that young man again but Mama blamed me for spending so much time in the old barn. Her blame when I was attacked or molested by a boy was a pattern that would follow me into adulthood.

And now, I was expelled from my private place too. Mama did not believe in her girl child having too much privacy, but she could not watch me all the time. I felt free to do what I wanted if I confessed in the confessional, my wants, and actions simply as, "I disobeyed my mother."

But the strange thing was I never questioned why she blamed me. Or why she seemed to believe or think I could control the wants of men?

As a child, I confessed the same sins every week, and when the priest asked me, "how many times?" I told him, "A hundred times, Father."

I did not want to lie and say once or twice, and a hundred seemed to cover the many sins I could not confess because they involved family secrets.

I tried to find new sins in the Little Examination of Conscience booklet that listed sins alphabetically, but the priest just laughed when I confessed, I committed adultery, "Do you know what that means, Jere?" I lied, but he knew, and I knew he knew. Now I was really in trouble. I had lied to a priest. And, he called me by name.

At first, Mama and Aunt Billie felt safer and happier in town.

Mother busied herself decorating the new house. She had made some money on the house trade and, for the first time, had a bit of cash for redecorating.

As sick as she was, she and Aunt Billie painted the white walls grey, and the chair molding the same deep red paisley that papered the bottom three feet of wall which made the furniture and house look like it came out of a designer magazine.

But we needed Billie's income to pay the bills and buy food. There were no government jobs that could pay her a salary she was accustomed to earning, and money was a constant concern.

Aunt Billie found a job with an architect in the town who also owned and operated the local paint store, which gave Mama a discount on the paint and wallpaper.

Daddy provided little or no help with money. When he left for work, he had taken a job at a drugstore in Lake Charles. I found a letter from that time where he explains to his sister, Virginia, he was determined to, "...hurt Winnie as she hurt me. She won't get any money from me. I will starve her out. See how she likes that?" He damn near did. But Mama had a will stronger than his and the ability to make do.

After Daddy moved to Lake Charles, he bought or borrowed a small Piper Cub airplane. He used us as an excuse saying he wanted to be closer to me and my brothers.

He would take Brother and me up and fly around St. Tammany Parish while he listened to baseball games. In between the pilot and passenger seat, he placed an ice chest loaded with his favorite Jax Beer and small Cokes or Barqs Root Beer for us.

One time when I was alone with him, he was drunk and spun out of control when he landed at a speed too fast for the gravel runway. I didn't get hurt but still carry the feeling of a plane tipping whenever I land on commercial flights.

Near the end of that summer in 1951, Mama sat Brother and me down and told us she and Daddy were getting a divorce.

I had to really think about that. *Divorce*, my parents divorced.

I took a long walk through town, past St. Peter's Catholic Church, and I said it aloud to myself, "My mama and daddy are divorced." Sr. Agatha said divorce was a mortal sin. But I knew my mother wasn't a mortal sinner, at least not about divorcing my daddy. I also knew divorce wasn't the sin; the sin was getting married again. I learned that fact in my *Baltimore Catechism*.

It made me sad, but I didn't cry. I thought the divorce was my fault because Daddy always said he loved me more than my mama. Later, I would come to realize he loved me and my brothers about the same way he loved Mama, which isn't saying much.

Two days after the divorce, Mama told us Daddy had married someone else. Then Mama told us we were moving out west where there were Indians, and it was warm and dry, and her lungs would get time to heal. By that point, the word *tuberculosis* was never mentioned anymore. She explained her extreme thinness and cough and need for rest were all due to "weak lungs."

Before we move, I remember sitting in the yard with her and Aunt Billie while they were taking a sunbathe.

Mama was wearing her two-piece chartreuse bathing suit and sitting on a towel in the yard with her knees drawn up to her chest. I could see her bones and the blue veins in her legs. It was the contrast between Aunt Billie's lush body and Mama's emaciated one that brought me to a moment of clarity.

I must have been staring because my mother turned to me and

asked what I was thinking. I couldn't tell her I had been thinking she was going to die and leave me like her mother did her. Aunt Billie must have seen it too because she said, "Let her be, Winnie. Everyone's entitled to their private thoughts."

Mama sold the house in town that we traded our real house on the river for. She used enough of the money from the sale to buy a new, red Studebaker convertible with red leather seats and a white canvas top. She sold most of our furniture and even more of our books. Then we packed up all the china and silver, the crystal, and the sacred cooking pots. We scheduled the drive west to begin on Thanksgiving Day.

The coming adventure distracted me from the pervading fear that Mama was going to die. I loved western movies and the look of mountains and desert landscapes. I was sure there would be plenty of horses to ride and Mama would get well, and we would never need to worry about her dying anymore.

I have no idea what my brother, Julian, was thinking. I didn't realize he would never be Brother anymore. Brother with whom I had played and fought disappeared on that terrible Easter Sunday when our father went crazy. My magical childhood was ending, and I needed to be ready for whatever the future brought into the new land. I didn't realize I was still only a child and didn't understand the greater world. Brother knew but he held it inside himself and would for many years.

Shortly before we left, Daddy came up the steps to the screened porch. I heard the screen door open and shut. I could see his silhouette against the glass panes of my door as he whispered to me to come away with him. It was extremely late. I didn't open it. I stood in front of it.

"What are you doing here, Daddy?" I knew he was drunk.

"Come on, little girl, you come with me where you belong."

"No, Daddy. I belong with Mama." Then I went and told my

Mother, but my father was gone by the time she went to see for herself.

CHAPTER 9
Fisherwoman

[1951]

On an early fall evening in 1951, we all drew together on the seawall in Mandeville at the north shore of Lake Ponchatrain.

In the motion picture part of my brain, the men, Uncle LC, and Whoo Paw built a fire and filled a large kettle with water from a hand pump. They set the pot on the burning logs while my young cousins Lucy and Susan and my little brother, Clay, played on the grassy area with its old moss-draped oaks, and Mama and her sisters walked out into the lake with a seine net stretched out between them.

Mama's long, dark hair hung free and thick with the soft, natural waves she could not control with all the crimps and curlers that filled her dressing table drawer. Her two-piece swimsuit hung on her thin frame, but the chartreuse, yellow, made her stand out from her sisters. She was the oldest and her bearing demanded attention even as her body wasted from tuberculosis.

Laura was the tallest of the three sisters. The shortest thing about her was her hips that made her legs and arms appear extra-long. She wore her chestnut hair in a long pageboy that was perfect in its correctness. She most resembled her mother, who was not a beauty nor elegant. Laura looked like a fine racehorse. Her swimsuit was from Hawaii, a brown, cotton print that spoke volumes about my godmother's innate sense of style.

Billie was the most voluptuous of the sisters. Everything about her was sexy and full, her lips, her breasts, and her hips that seemed to rise away from a perfectly portioned waistline. But she did everything she could to make her body disappear behind a dull, black swimsuit that erased her wonderful curves and freedom of movement. She covered her hair with an old scarf that made me think of the nuns at St. Peters on Saturdays when they wore their short, denim, work veils.

Ellen wore white. Her long, blonde hair pulled tight away from her face by French braids that caught up the short strands of new growth and wove them into a single, long braid that hung behind her head and down her back. Ellen was the most petite of the sisters and the most naturally beautiful.

As the sun set behind my mother and my aunts, they held the net between them, pulling it toward shore, scooping into it crabs, shrimp and small, flapping fish. I remember their strong arms pulling in unison, their bodies operating as one.

When the net was full, they brought their catch up to the sea wall and culled out the smallest fish and the female crabs that carried eggs inside their fibrous sacks. As the sun sank into the western horizon of the lake and the moon rose into the sky, we children sat with our mothers and aunts and ate the warm seafood the women had caught, and the men had cooked.

In an album from the 1980s I find photos of me in my yellow swimsuit top and cutoff jeans running through the surf at north Padre Island. I notice that sheathed to my leg is the sharp knife I used to cut smelly bait and the cord needed to tie it onto ring nets before I could hang them from the pier.

During that time my children fish with their father as I

become the fisherwoman who emerges from the river of memory. I provide my family with the bounty of my catch and we cook it in the old aluminum pot that belonged to my husband's grandmother, Angelina Profumo Cusimano.

In these newer memories, I cook the crabs I capture. The ones my children never find too much trouble to crack open and peel. Their fingers digging into the hard, red shells, pulling the morsels of soft, white flesh into their mouths as their clenched teeth draw in the coarser claw meat that is striped with brown. They swallow the mixture of flesh whole.

CHAPTER 10

Ruby

I was afraid that Ruby wouldn't come anymore when we moved to town.
     But she helped us pack one house and unpack the other. And on the first Sunday afternoon in the new house, there she was with her old tin pie plate. She cranked our ice cream every Sunday afternoon that summer and fall.

The Sunday before we left, I took Ruby's plate of food out to her and later, while she cranked the ice cream, standing before her, I shifted from foot to foot. I couldn't stand it anymore. I couldn't leave without knowing. I told her the secret Mama told me about Chicago and Ruby's uppity husband and the baby being killed by the white trash mob and how I was sure they had to drag the baby off her tit, with milk still clinging to his little mouth and then I was crying and telling her how sorry I was.

Ruby just looked at me with those same, sad eyes that always looked like they were crying or about to.

She never stopped cranking that ice cream, as she reached out with her free hand and touched my face, wiping away the tears.

Then, holding my face firm between the snuff-covered fingers of her large hand she said, "I never went to Chicago, girl. You don't have to go away from this town to lose your family or get beat up. Don't you know that girl? Now here, you put the salt on the ice. Be careful now. That's right. You're doing fine, Miss Jere, just fine."

CHAPTER 11

San Juan Ranch

[1951]

We left Covington on Thanksgiving Day, 1951. The new red Studebaker packed to the gills. Mama rode in the passenger seat while Aunt Billie did the driving. Clay was now a tall, skinny toddler, as he rode between them, seated on top of the padded red leather map box, looking like a lookout on a pirate ship.

Julian and I sat in the back seat with our feet propped up on luggage. The seat between us was covered in comic books. The trunk was full. Besides clothes, we carried Mama's bean and roux pot, alchemical starch, ice cream custard, spaghetti, the fudge pot, and the silver. Mama did not like to eat with stainless. She didn't trust the movers too much either.

"Hide your eyes, children."

"Slow down Billie! Oh my God, we are going to fall off this mountain. Don't look children."

"For God's sake, Winnie, why don't you hide your eyes? You're distracting me and scaring the kids."

"Ohhhh! Mother of Mercy, please allow us to survive this trial ... Too fast, Billie. Slow down."

"Winnie, there is a line of cars a mile long behind me."
"Let them wait!"
The road west was a rocky one.

In a small, nameless, west Texas town, Mama locked the keys in the trunk of the Studebaker. No one in the town had ever seen or worked on a Studebaker, and it took hours for a locksmith from another town to arrive and retrieve the only set of keys.

Mama had carefully packed the extra set in the top drawer of the buffet that sat in storage till we found a place to live.

Then there was the matter of the coffee. No one on the road was willing to boil Mama's milk for her coffee. To say she had an attitude doesn't even touch how she approached the wait staff and owners of the small eating establishments we stopped at along the roads out west. She was forced to drink coffee with cream from the small pitchers outraged waitresses slapped down on the tables where we sat.

Food was another matter. Mama declared the Mexican restaurants were dirty, and the food was not to be trusted; American food wasn't the same as in the south, where they served grits with your eggs instead of potatoes and the iced tea was sweet. Even the clientele was called into question. We had to leave one restaurant when I pointed out:

"Look, there's a colored family sitting over there."

"Don't point your finger and lower your voice."

"We're hungry Mama, why can't we stay?"

"Gentry from Louisiana do not sit in a restaurant that serves coloreds."

"We'll just have to make do."

Mama bought a loaf of soft, white bread and a jar of peanut butter and apple jelly.

Nothing in the west measured up to the way things were done in Louisiana. Nothing was proper or like home. And we had to save money, so we only took one room at the dismal travel courts we stayed in, all of us crowding onto the same bed laying crosswise.

Our arrival in Santa Fe was dismal. It was cold and damp, and we crowded into two small rooms of a travel court next to the tiny river that flowed through the town.

Loretto Academy, which would be my new school after Christmas break, was across the bridge from the travel court. Since our trip had taken longer than she planned, Mama decided it would be best if Julian and I took the rest of the semester off. We did not object.

There was a hot plate and cubbyhole with a small counter, a sink and shelves in the cabin that had been advertised as having a kitchen. Since they had not had any decent or home cooked food since leaving Louisiana, Mama and Aunt Billie started a pot of red beans. The next day the boiling beans were still hard. Later, they would discover baking soda helped beans cook in high altitude, but by then they had lost their enthusiasm for conquering the vicissitudes of mountain life.

A short article from the March 1952 edition of the New Mexico newspaper sums up the Santa Fe experience for the sisters:

> "The popular and attractive New Orleans sisters, Winifred R. Smith, and Billie R. Eustis, are leaving next week to take a house in Phoenix, Arizona for the remainder of the winter. They were in residence here at San Juan Ranch until being snowed in a few times, thence were at home on the Camino where they've continued to struggle against the elements in a stormy winter that's made ski enthusiasts happy but not these visitors from the South."

What the article doesn't say is how totally out of their element the sisters were. It wasn't just the snow or the mountain roads, or the dark-skinned strangeness of the Mexicans and Indians. They just weren't prepared for the most outrageous difference from the south.

There was a freedom in the West that terrified my mother and aunt. The social crowd didn't seem to care whose people's families were. They didn't care about what a person did in the past if they were interesting and fun in the now. The sisters wanted to have fun but lacked the courage of their desire. They could not break free from the strictures of their upbringing.

None of our coats were suitable for the frigid winter. The only store they could afford was the Sears Outlet where items could be ordered from the catalogue.

They did find two natural camel hair short coats hanging on a rack in the store at $3.50 each. They bought them in one size that fits all adults, expecting me to grow into them since I turned eleven that winter.

But I wore Mama's old maroon coat instead. It's fabric was thin and too long for me but with a sweater it made do. I looked and felt ridiculous. Mama said I was building my character by not worrying about what other people, "who didn't matter anyway," think.

"We just have to make do for now, Jere."

Before leaving Covington, a friend of Mama's, who also had tuberculosis, recommended the mountain city of Santa Fe as a healing place. She gave Mama the names of Dude Ranches or small hotels whose owners might want caretakers for the winter.

During the first week in Santa Fe, Mama and Aunt Billie contacted the owners of San Juan Ranch situated in the foothills above the town. My mother and aunt agreed to spend the winter as the caretakers of the ranch while the owners wintered in New Orleans. In return, we got to live rent-free. There was no physical work required as the partners had a Mexican couple come in weekly to clean and maintain the property and roads.

The owners were two single and charming men from New Orleans. I remember they were tall and extroverted. They encouraged mother and Aunt Billie by saying that every problem with mountain life could be managed. Then while pointing toward the horizon they explained that the school bus would stop at the base of the property.

There was a short cut over land instead of the red clay road that wound around the mountain. What we all missed were the rocks and cliffs that Julian and I would have to traverse to get to the roadway.

Before they set off the owners showed us how Clay and I could share a room in the main lodge and Julian could have a room outside the kitchen. They also introduced me to their two large poodles, Pierre, and Collette.

I loved the ranch. A small room off the kitchen was a bar decorated with a canopy and high bar stools that became my room for daydreaming and reading. It reminded me of my daddy and was private.

No one else spent time in the bar that was just a hallway connecting the living quarters to the large, sunken grand parlor and the kitchen. Mama was slowly recuperating from her tuberculosis and the divorce from Daddy. But the isolation of the ranch was profound. It brought Mama back to the house on Military Road during the time of the terror.

Only now we had two large poodles to function as guard dogs. But our new nocturnal visitors were not mysterious intruders but brown bears that liked to snoop around the house at night for warmth and food. When we woke in the mornings we caught a whiff of their wild scent which always lingered.

. . .

Another problem that developed soon after we moved in arrived with the first snow. The red clay road that wound its way from the highway to the ranch would become icy so the Studebaker didn't have the weight or power to hold traction on it. This was a problem we couldn't have anticipated since the weather was dry when we first visited and moved into the ranch.

The housekeeper arrived with her husband in their battered old car and a set of chains for our tires. But with great disdain, the husband pronounced mother's prize possession a piece of useless machinery. Once more, mama had to depend on the kindness of the dark-skinned people she held in contempt.

Every room had a fireplace, and the owners left us with several cords of mesquite logs and branches. The sections of the ceilings between the great beams were like the surface waves of an ocean and the shadows from the fires made it seem like we were floating beneath the ocean. Did any of us know the land and mountains were made of sandstone and had once been the bed of a great ocean?

The impractical aspects of San Juan Ranch were overcome, at least for me, by the stark beauty of the patio outside the large picture window in the living quarters. It had a view of the distant mesas and the covered walkways that connected the Rancho buildings. It was the land of adobe, sandstone, and red clay.

At a Christmas party the sisters attended, the discussion revolved around the owners of the ranch. Mama and Aunt Billie discovered the charming men from New Orleans were queer. Mama's term, not mine.

Then Mama noticed the beams that separated the waves of the ceilings were splitting. They had long, vertical cracks. Not believing when friends tried to reassure her the splits were normal, and sure we would all be crushed under their weight, Mama sent for our furniture from storage.

I remember spending Christmas at the ranch but before the start of school in early January we moved into a small rental house on Camino road. It was a house at the end of the road, owned by a real family with a mother and father and a giant playroom for their young son who became my best and only friend during our short stay.

Years later, Aunt Billie told me my mother was having a nervous breakdown during that brief time of isolation in the mountains.

"We couldn't afford a doctor. She really needed a psychiatrist, so I became her analyst. Her artist friend Miriam in Covington told us all about her own struggles and, of course, your mother read articles about them. She was highly intelligent and curious. We, however, were both concerned about losing our minds back then. I promised her she could tell me anything and I wouldn't ever throw it back at her. So, every evening as the light disappeared, we got you kids to leave us alone and we sat in the small sitting room next to the bar and talked over bourbons and water."

I have this vision of the two of them sitting alone on a backless sofa, drinks in hand, looking out a large window that looked out over the mountains toward the distant mesas, softly talking while we kids waited to be called to dinner.

And even before Billie's dementia became evident, I knew that stopping my aunt's reflections on Mama would immediately close her down, raise the wall between us and shut me out. Collecting snippets of her memory, I bided my time waiting for what, I knew not, but I trusted there was something important hidden behind Billie's eyes that clouded over as she spoke about the past.

When I think back to Santa Fe and being a young girl in the early 1950s, the things I remember are the exotica of the plaza square where I stared at the Native American women sitting on blankets selling beaded jewelry with their papooses close by.

But what I remember most was the red clay. Most of the streets were unpaved and, because of the constantly melting snow, the roads filled with ruts from car tires. There were no sidewalks in the neighborhoods. My new saddle oxfords and white socks turned to the color of rust. When we drew water from the faucet, we had to allow the red clay to settle down to the bottom of the glass before drinking. All our drinking glasses turned orange and had to be thrown away when we moved from the mountain town I had come to love.

The Santa Fe Opera is now located on the grounds of the old San Juan Ranch.

On one of my yearly solitary trips to New Mexico during my fifties, sixties, I visited the property. The executive offices were in the old ranch house. Since it was out of season, I was allowed to tour the original building.

I had forgotten about the wave effect of the ceilings, but everything else was exactly as I remembered. The only significant difference was the road leading to the ranch. It's paved now and no longer winds around the mountain. A major highway cuts through the mountain and the road to the opera company is more like a driveway. But then my more recent memories are not as clear as those from childhood.

CHAPTER 12

Good Mothers

In January 1952, I entered my new school, Loretto Academy. The principal was the young and beautiful Sister that Mama and I had met with at the required interview for admittance. She had given Mama a list of the uniform requirements as well as a supply list.

I remember the interview and the list: navy blue and white oxfords; white blouses with Peter Pan collars; navy blue skirts preferably pleated; navy blue sweaters; and binders with small lines and blue ink. Mama took the list and promptly threw it out.

"Who do they think they are? Education is important, not what you wear. Do they think everyone is as rich as those foreigners who board there?"

Indeed, many of the boarders were girls from wealthy, Latin American families. So were many of our neighbors. I thought they were Mexican. Their lineage in New Mexico stretched back for hundreds of generations.

One of my classmates lived on a street on the way to the school. She invited me to visit her. There was an adobe outer wall surrounding the house and an enclosed courtyard. I remember the courtyard with its brilliant blue exterior doorway; and the clay tiles; and pots planted with cactus and succulents in the nooks and crannies of the exterior walls of the house.

Did Mama not understand the architecture of her beloved French Quarter in New Orleans was Spanish in design? That it could have just as well become the Spanish Quarter? Or was Spain, okay? Would she still have been repulsed by these brown-skinned people who rolled their r's and planted cacti instead of flowers in the sandy soil where they lived? Did she not realize that Native American tribes built the trail that became Military Road that named our river, the Bogue Falaya?

On my first day of class, the principal looked at my mismatched outfit.

I wore the Kelly-green sweater and brown and white saddle oxfords my mother had given me that Christmas at San Juan Ranch. I wore a new straight collar, white blouse instead of the suggested Peter Pan collar. I held an old, blue binder with wide-lined paper instead of the suggested narrow-lined. Looking back, it was the bottle of green ink that really caused the principal to smile at me and say ever so softly, "Oh, I see."

Sometime in late January or early February, Mama, and Aunt Billie and my brothers drove to Phoenix, Arizona to find us a new home and left me in the care of the Loretto Sisters.

The Sisters gave me a room of my own with a door leading to a balcony over the front of the building that overlooked the street and the iron fence in front of the chapel. A light shone in the window and cast shadows on the walls of my room. It reminded me of the yellow plaid room with the porch I had loved until my daddy came knocking on the door. But in this room, I felt safe.

The sisters taught me the value of making my own order by making the bed every morning, changing the sheets on Saturdays, washing out my underwear before bed, brushing my teeth and washing my face with soap and water before bed and on rising.

On the first Monday after I arrived as a boarder, it was my dorm's turn to go to Mass in the Chapel of Loretto. I remember it was snowing, and we had warm coats on. But once inside, the comfort of the candles and the lights and sacred smells of incense made my body turn very warm as I struggled out of my coat and tucked it under the seat in front of me. The younger Sisters were standing on the spiral staircase that led to the choir loft where all the nuns who were not supervising students were chanting in Latin. The choir loft was high over the pews, and the ceiling seemed to rise to the sky.

The chapel windows were the brilliant blue that I now see in waves as I fall asleep. Right next to my pew, a white statue of Jesus with open arms pointed downward stood on a white pedestal.

Shortly after Mass began, I felt funny. The lights were shimmering, and my whole body was tingling, and I heard a buzzing sound in my ears. At first, I thought it was because Jesus was going to whisper something to me.

But then I realized, "I'm going to faint. This is what fainting feels ..."

The next thing I knew, the principal who had looked at my outfit on the first day of school that January was kneeling next to me as she whispered, "You fainted, Jere. Do you think you could stand if I help you?"

I loved these Sisters, who were called by the title of *Mother*, and who recognized and praised my ability to read aloud. And who never, to my knowledge, ever hit a child.

I was in awe of the elderly and regal Mother Superior who allowed me to choose two dark chocolate-covered cherry candies from the box on her desk the Saturday mornings when I boarded.

The boarders had two free times a day during the week. The first, in the afternoons following study hall, allowed us to play in the school yard or to play board games inside if the weather was too cold. I didn't have any friends among the other boarders. I was short term and new. It was late in the year, and everyone knew I would be leaving soon, so I was hardly worth getting to know.

Homesick for the Bogue Falaya River and the tall pines of Southeast Louisiana, I am drawn to the river that runs across the street from the brick wall and gate I enter every day as a day student.

Boarders could not leave the grounds without permission, something I'm sure would be denied, so I never ask. The river became like my daddy's gun closet, a forbidden place where I could find a piece of what I longed for. In this case, home.

Every afternoon I would pass through the gate and climb down the embankment to the shallow water whose bed was filled with stones instead of clean, loose sand and looked more like a large ditch than a river. Instead of tall pines, its banks were lined with cottonwood trees and other smaller trees I could walk through and sit among.

On one of my excursions, I found a small basket sitting on the edge of the water. As I picked it up, my imagination took flight. I was sure the basket belonged to a Native American woman who had used it to hold the clothes she washed in the river. But I had never seen any of the women from the Plaza wash clothes in the river and I knew the basket was too small.

Then I imagined the basket was the holder of a baby, an abandoned baby, like baby Moses sent down the river to be found by a good princess. I even searched the bank for a baby.

All the while, I held the basket close to my chest. I wanted that basket. It felt soft, warm, and new. I looked around to see if anyone stood watching or if the owner was nearby so I could return it. Not seeing anyone, I hid it underneath my coat and sneaked back into the gate of the convent. Surely the Sisters were watching me from the upper floor of their residence. No one ever asked me about my afternoon visits to the river, nor did anyone ever question the basket I hid in the back of the closet next to my bed.

We also had free time the hour before bed. On my first evening, one of the older nuns asked, "Jere, I hear you're having trouble with long division."

"Yes, Mother, I just can't figure it out. I'm not good at arithmetic." I felt ashamed to be so stupid. No one else seemed to have so much trouble.

"While you're here, I can help you. I taught mathematics for many years." Mathematics was something high school students studied. How was she going to teach me?

"Will you let me help you? Are you willing to give up your free time to do more work?"

"I guess, Mother, but I just don't understand it." Another Sister, even older than my soon-to-be-math teacher, walked up.

"Jere, I hear you like to sew." How did these nuns know so much about me?

"Yes, Mother, a little. A baby-sitter taught me to cross stitch on pillowcases."

"Do you use a thimble?"

"No, Mother. I tried to use my grandmother's, but it kept falling off."

"I'm sure I can find one to fit. I can show you."

These two retired teachers had a mission. They were like our old maid, Betty. Failure was not an option. I would work with the math teacher and when I felt tired or got frustrated, the sewing nun would take over.

She had me practice pushing the needle with the thimble, over and over. As I mastered the thimble, she taught me to darn a worn sock stretched over a wooden egg, using yarn to weave a patch, my middle finger pushing the needle like a shuttle. Then she taught me to replace buttons onto my uniform blouses. Like the back-

and-forth weaving stitches, these two sisters taught me math and sewing, both necessary skills to develop independence.

Did they know how they were engaging both my mind and my body? Was it planned or a mere accident?

Our fifth-grade teacher at the Academy read books to our class each day for half an hour after lunch. We would put our heads on our arms crossed over our desks and rest while she read *Tom Sawyer, Huckleberry Finn,* and *Little Women*. These brief sessions increased my longing to read as I listened and waited each day for the next segment. Shortly before I left the Sisters, I called *Mother*, and before we moved away, we started to read a new book, Little Men. Leaving then left me with the sense of an unfinished musical composition stopped in mid-stanza.

Shortly after the move in April 1952, I entered my first public school and third school in fifth grade and learned I was not a failure.

On a pop quiz, I correctly answered all the long division and multiplication problems. At the new school there were no letter grades, you were graded: Satisfactory, Fair or Unsatisfactory.

On the first day there, I met my new best friend, Vicki. She was Jewish. The only things I knew about Jews at that point in time was what the first group of nuns in Covington taught, that they, the Jews, killed Jesus. Vicki assured me that was not true, and by the time we had that discussion, it didn't matter to me, because I couldn't believe that such nice people would do such a thing.

When I brought her home to meet my mother, I learned Vicki was not welcome. But when I met her family, they welcomed me like a long-lost sister to their daughter.

My mother's refusal to welcome my new friend didn't matter. She and I became almost inseparable as we played jacks and jump rope and hopscotch in her back patio and ate the marvelous food her mother cooked for family and friends.

Vicki showed me the way to the small public library located in a shady area of nearby Encanto Park.

On its shelves I found a copy of *Little Men*. I read my way back to the page where the Sister had stopped. I was no longer in chaos. My fear of school was replaced with the excitement and curiosity I had lost upon entering kindergarten.

And more than that, my education was expanding my understanding of what was true and what was a lie.

CHAPTER 13

Good Sisters

On the trip to find a new home, Mama had bought a small house for us in the Encanto Park area of Phoenix.

Outside it was a simple red brick ranch house. But inside it had beautiful windows cut into the interior brick walls. It was filled with designer touches and constructed to keep the house comfortable with a giant cooler that allowed cool air to flow into the barely cracked windows throughout.

The living room had two exterior walls made with three large rectangular windows that had trap doors near the ground to allow air to flow into the large living room that went all the way to the back wall, which was constructed with the same windows.

The long interior wall was made of concrete blocks forming a lovely, checkered design.

In the front area of the large room stood a small fireplace hidden behind a screen attached to the wall. The kitchen which protruded into the back section of the large room was hidden behind wood paneling and glass blocks that let in light, but hid the small room where Mama and Aunt Billie prepared all our meals and where Julian and I baked cakes that never went to waste.

It was a real brick house. The walls painted with the soft colors of the Arizona desert I would come to love.

The most distinctive feature of the house, at least on our block, were the concrete floors, driveway, walkway, and patio, that were all stained a deep red and highly polished. It became my job to mop those floors every afternoon with a barely damp mop, so they kept their shine. Julian was responsible for cutting the grass and hosing down the driveway and patio.

Julian and I both got our own rooms. Clay slept with our mother during the five years we spent in Phoenix.

Billie liked to sleep alone, and there was a worry about her getting tuberculosis since she already had bronchial problems. But the real reason for the sleeping arrangements was Aunt Billie's new job at Edwards Airforce Base. She had to leave well before dawn to make the drive into the desert. She bedded down by eight every night, first laying out her clothes, so she wouldn't wake us. The consequence was we all had to be in our rooms ready for bed by eight o'clock.

Julian's bedroom had a door to the backyard so we could slip in and out when there was a school event.

Our next-door neighbor, Ms. Basler, was an early pioneer of the Arizona territory.

I remember she wore blue shirtwaist dresses with beautiful turquoise and silver jewelry. Her bracelets ran up her arms and her chest was adorned with priceless pieces of Native American art.

She was thick around her middle, but it didn't matter because she was long wasted and had beautiful, long grey hair that she wound into braids around her head. Her face and skin were dry and wrinkled from years in the desert air. But her back yard was an oasis of shade.

I'm not sure how she accomplished the shade. Her yard was

less deep than ours or perhaps her house was set back from the street more than the neighboring houses or it's possible the shade was merely a glitch in my memory.

She had a television, and we only had a radio. She was generous and welcomed us into her home to watch unique events like the Coronation of Queen Elisabeth II and the Republican National Convention nomination of Dwight Eisenhower. Mama was telling complete strangers to be sure and vote for Ike and felt like she had helped bring him into the fold. She considered Adlai Stevenson a communist and would only hear of the candidacy of Ike to carry the Republican Banner.

Tuesday nights, the Bishop Fulton Sheen, whose show *Life is Worth Living,* kept my mother and aunt enthralled with his elegance and intelligence, which always seemed to agree with their world view. Mrs. Basler and my aunt loved Friday night wrestling, particularly Gorgeous George, a short-lived personality who stole the hearts of women as he dressed in elegant fur lined, long capes finished with sequins. Mama thought he was coarse. But by then we all knew she lacked a sense of humor.

As Ms. Basler grew afraid to be alone, she hired me to spend nights with her. She paid me fifty cents a night and allowed me to watch the sitcoms and dramatic shows. But the best part of staying with her was the stories of her adventures as a young child heading west on a wagon train.

My favorite story was about the time they crossed an area of soft desert sand. The wagons carried long boards that were used as emergency roadbeds. But even with the help of the boards, the horses and mules could not pull the heavy wagons loaded with family belongings. The most precious commodities were water and food.

As I listened, I thought of all the things we left behind in Louisiana, a tall pine plantation desk, the iron twin beds Brother and I shared, so many of Mama's books, my Nanee's old rocker that had sat in the hallway of the house on Military Road next to the big wooden radio that sat on her sewing machine. All of it is gone. But not from memory.

Like death, I had to hold on to the memory. But that's the problem of childhood memories, they are fragmented like the shards of a broken mirror. And that's what I have been doing all these years, taking to finishing this book. Fitting the pieces together.

Daddy wasn't paying child support. The first summer, we drove back to Louisiana to make him pay.

Mama kept saying she was going to throw him in jail, but her friends cautioned her not to talk that way in front of the children. Julian and I were used to Mama saying things she never followed through on. She still couldn't work, and we needed new shoes and school clothes. But part of her wanted to go back to Louisiana to tell her friends and family and the good colored to vote for a Republican, as Louisiana was still a Democratic State. I have no memory of her being political before our move west, except her hatred for the Long family.

The thing I most remember about that trip back home was I almost drowned. We visited Mama's friends, the Percys, who lived upriver from us.

The adults were drinking early afternoon bourbons, and we children went down to swim in their river. The path was longer than our part was. Not paying attention, I stepped into a hole and sank. My lungs filled with water and my brain did this thing where I felt euphoric. As a young child, when I thought about death and what people said, like your whole life events passed through your mind when you died. My thoughts were immediate.

"I'm drowning and it doesn't hurt. It feels good." And just as I was growing comfortable with dying, the oldest girl from the family we visited grabbed my hair and pulled me up, shouting "You silly girl! You were drowning yourself." I know now why that near-death experience by accidental drowning was so memorable. I mistook the euphoria I felt for the feeling of being overwhelming love. And I began to seek that feeling in a lot of ways, both good and bad.

Shortly after summer was over, and I began sixth grade, I had my first period. I was still eleven and Mama was shocked my menses began so early.

I had terrible cramps, so I stayed in bed with a hot water bottle, missing school for the first two days of my periods each month. Mama said the cramps were God's way of preparing me for childbirth. She must have talked to other women about the early onset of my menstrual and learned it wasn't unusual in the desert. I don't know if it appeased her dislike of the west or added to her distaste even though the heat and climate were finally healing her lungs.

But the pain and missing school gave me time to think about the things I was learning in class.

The pain taught me how to dissociate from it by reading, so I always had stacks of library books on hand. I remember reading the *Diary of Anne Frank* and being enthralled by how similar her experiences were to mine. I felt connected to this little Jewish girl who was hidden away in the back of a house, feeling isolated from her family, just like I was hidden away inside of myself. I think my friendship with Vicki and her family added to the feeling of connection.

By then, I was beginning to understand how isolated Mama felt. She had no friends her age anymore. And the lack had nothing to do with her fear of germs or theirs.

I remember when I met a girl my age shortly after moving into our new home. Her mother was genuinely nice and happy to find out my family was Catholic until she discovered my parents divorced and my mother's sister lived with us. Suddenly, I wasn't welcome anymore and my newfound friend was never free to play. I was living in a neighborhood of children and feeling more isolated than ever.

I now called my older brother Julian'instead of Brother, but he was not anything like the big brother I had known in Louisiana.

He withdrew and became selfish and mean. I was not allowed to read his books though, of course, I did. He no longer played games with me. I wasn't allowed around his friends. He shouted, "No talking!" if the rest of us talked during dinner.

Now, I realize he was just an unhappy, teenage boy filled with rage, whose teachers didn't understand his intelligence, forcing him to try the Military to find his place in the world. Mama let him get away with his boorish behavior and because he was a boy, he didn't have to help clean the kitchen or do any housekeeping chores. As she prepared him for adulthood, the chores were all left to me. I missed my big brother terribly.

Julian became obsessed with the ROTC program at his high school. His commander was a good man who saw he needed discipline and a role where he could succeed.

My brother's old obsession with building model airplanes subsided as he spread out some newspaper to polish his boots and shoes and clean his rifle. He learned to sew on his own merit badges with tiny, almost invisible stitches. He made friends for the first time since leaving Louisiana. And he rose in rank so that by the end of his junior year, he was part of the leadership team.

Without a big brother to talk to during that time, I listened to the radio shows featuring true romance and true confessions while I cleaned house and watched out for Clay during long summer days.

I developed a fantasy life where I was an orphan forced into labor to get food and a bed.

In sixth grade, I wrote my father, begging him to visit me. I began to fantasize he would come to see me and hold me in his arms. My fantasy was, I was his little girl.

Finally, a typed letter from Daddy arrived telling me he couldn't get away because he and Boots had a new little baby girl, a true beauty. Her name was Cindy. I hid the letter in the basket I found in Santa Fe as a way of hiding my hurt. Mama often called Daddy a bastard, and I really didn't want to hear her go into a rage about him. There was so much to be careful about with my mother.

She knew I played with Vicki whenever I could leave to have time for myself, but I couldn't talk to her or any of my family about our friendship.

Increasingly, my life or the things and people whom I needed had to be kept secret or at least not discussed. I couldn't bring my questions about beliefs to them or talk about things I was learning in school that might bring disapproval. Clay was the only one I might have talked to, and he was too young, so I sought comfort alone in my room and talked about things to myself.

I certainly couldn't talk to Vicki or her parents about how I had to keep my friendship with them to myself. It became a real barrier to becoming the real me because, like so many children, I had to split myself in half. And it made me hyper-vigilant, least I make a mistake as I often did in my enthusiasm to express wonder at my own developing ideas that didn't fit within the accepted boundaries of whatever group I was speaking to or engaged with. And the worst thing was feeling like there was never and would never be someone I could explore with.

School became my outlet. The English teacher, Miss Blue, painted the walls of her classroom in the colors of desert sky at dawn and sunset, and in one corner of her classroom was a real desert garden of sand and cacti.

She had us read the diary of Helen Keller. For a week, we wrote paragraphs each day about the sensory experience of sunrise. On Tuesday morning we woke at dawn and were instructed to close our eyes and listen.

The next day, to open our eyes and hold our hands over our ears or stuff them with cotton. All this to stimulate our awareness of our different senses.

The feel of the cool air on our skin, early morning scents, the sound of birds and crickets, and the glory of the desert sunrise. And it taught me to become a descriptive writer. By eighth grade, we read the epic poems of Wordsworth and the simple stanzas of Emily Dickinson.

All my teachers opened windows into a world of ideas and language.

We had a music teacher once a week who told us stories of the great operas and taught us to hum or sing the themes as he played them on a portable record player. He played the Grand Canyon Suite so we could integrate the music into our bodies and hear it when we were in the desert or went with our families to see the great wonder itself.

I learned that La Bohemme had three themes:, tuberculosis, love and death.

Each year in my public school got better. Starting in sixth grade, we had sex education. We also had ballroom dance lessons and were separated by gender so we could learn about our bodies.

In eighth grade, our principal Mr. Oswald came into our classrooms to teach deportment. It was part of sexuality. He had us role play the good manners of dating couples as we acted out young men opening the car door and waiting for the girls to exit. Young men held out the chair for the girl and waited for her to be seated at the dining table before sitting.

Young ladies were to always say "thank you" and take care not to order the most expensive item on the menu. That always brought laughter because none of the boys had any money. Girls could, at least, babysit. We were being prepared for our future etiquette. And respect for each other.

In eighth grade, two subjects were required in Arizona to complete grade school.

Half the year was devoted to the history of the United States Constitution and the Bill of Rights. We studied and read the documents, about the period, and about the men and women who were part of its development. Then we had debates and argued the finer points of the Constitution and its effect on the citizens of the United States. We even held moot court trials.

I realized that the Constitution, like the *Baltimore Catechism*, taught me to reflect on laws and the questions I had as I struggled to understand the meaning behind the words and what it all meant in real time.

In the second half of the year, we studied Arizona History and the western movement.

We created a papiermâché map of the United States. It filled half the classroom with our desks surrounding it. I learned that the experiences of my next-door neighbor, Ms. Basler, were part of the universal struggles of the pioneers who left their homes behind and moved to these desert lands. And more importantly, we, our classmates and teachers, were part of the still ongoing history.

We learned about the Arizona State Constitution and Government that was modeled on the U.S. Constitution but held to the unique qualities that land, and water use in the desert states required.

We also learned about the different Indian tribes in Arizona, but I do not remember learning about the Indian Wars that were fought across the West. The only thing I knew about those struggles I learned through watching movies. But I still had a lot to learn. This was all just the toe hold.

. . .

The best things about Encanto were my teachers. The men wore jeans, as they taught us science and math and the geology of California and Arizona.

They found the money for microscopes and taught us how to use them, as well as provided bugs and gels with microorganisms so we could identify them. They made science interesting and fun.

They showed us the now infamous films about the atomic bomb explosions and scenarios of what would happen if the Russians should bomb us. We got on our knees under the desks for the bomb drills, with everyone farting and laughing because our school was built as a campus system. All the doors led to the outside and every classroom had a wall of windows on the far side of the rooms.

At home, Aunt Billie bought us a set of encyclopedias that included the "great short stories of the Western World."

The deal also included subscriptions to *The Saturday Evening Post* and *Life* magazines, a *Ladies Home Companion Cookbook* and a leather-bound copy of the Bible in living color.

The Bible disintegrated long ago, but the cookbook remains a used household item.

Meanwhile the world of politics was offered to me via the magazines and Ms. Basler's television. She allowed me to watch the Joseph McCarthy hearings that were televised during the day at the end of seventh grade and into the summer of 1954.

I was becoming educated in both the house of my mother and my Catholic Church. I wanted to please them both, but I could not stop developing my own thoughts as I explored innovative ideas and arrived at my own judgements.

CHAPTER 14

The Turn of the Screw

In seventh grade, our Catholic Church held Confirmation classes. I attended them and met a girl who would become my new best friend. Her last name was Augustine. She came from a wonderful family of three daughters and a boy about Clay's age.

Her father was always reading the newspaper, and her mother was warm, comfortable and comforting, and left us alone. Her oldest daughter was married, but my friend had a sister just a year older. The three of us became fast friends as we practiced becoming women. Not "ladies" mind you, "women."

We played with cheap cosmetics left behind by the married sister. Old shoe boxes filled with tiny sample lipstick colors and ten-cent bottles of nail polish became our treasures as we tried on colors and practiced kissing our arms until they bruised. My mother forbade this kind of play because it was sexual. But I was becoming a sexual being and there was no way to stop it.

I started smoking and stealing cigarettes from open packs left on tables by Mama and Aunt Billie. It made me vomit, but believing smoking was sophisticated, I stayed with it.

. . .

After the promise of spring, when I was confirmed in May, came summer. And the summer of 1954 was not a good summer.

I was, free of sin, mature in faith, and I had almost convinced my mother to allow me to attend the Catholic school my last year of grade school because I had become very fond of the Sister who taught eighth grade and my confirmation class.

I thought that with her help, I would stay in a constant state of perfect grace, adored in the eyes of God, my family, and my new friends. However, that same summer between seventh and eighth grade, I was assaulted by a boy in the alleyway near my house.

Shortly before Vicki moved from Phoenix to California without saying goodbye, disaster struck in the form of a fat, pimpled face, flat-topped hair boy on a blue rider bicycle.

I was on my way to buy a soft drink and get some air in my old, rusted bike's tires, when halfway through the alleyway, he rode up from the opposite direction. He smiled and called out to me to stop.

This was a boy who had never directly spoken to me. He and his friends would shout insults about my hair, my small breasts, the way I spoke, held my head and the stupid clothes I wore, and of course, my buck teeth. However, with his smile, the insults and hurts were forgotten, and forgiven. My new-found pureness of soul was shining through to the outside. Finally, I was attractive. I stopped.

He moved his bicycle up next to mine and suddenly pulled my arms down and under my handlebars, and then turned them up around his bike, locking us in an embrace of metal and flesh. Then he stuck his tongue into my mouth. In that moment, I knew my state of grace was over. It was grief. I had worked so hard to find my grace and now it was being taken away.

I screamed, cried, pulled, and tried to kick myself free. Surely, someone heard my screams, but no one came. Most mothers didn't work, only divorced mothers like mine.

The boy had to let my hands go free so he could slap me in the face. Then he pushed me hard down to the ground and rode away.

I pulled myself up. My skin was torn from the asphalt and where the bikes had cut into me. My lip was bleeding, and I had a bloody nose where the handlebar hit me when I fell. As I sped home in hysterics, my body was filling with shame.

Julian was holding his ROTC leaders meeting. The living room was filled with older boys and the Army Sergeant who was the unit's faculty advisor. Hoping they wouldn't notice, I covered my face with my hands as I ran through the room and into my mother's bedroom and under her bed. There, I curled up into a fetal position, trying desperately to disappear back into myself, just knowing the attack was my fault. I was sure that the boy knew how evil and bad I was, that he could sense and smell I was vile, sinful, and disgusting. Then there were faces and voices surrounding me.

Kneeling on the floor, peering under the bed were my brother, the sergeant, and the student commander I had a secret crush on.

"Come out, Jere. We won't hurt you," they coaxed. I screamed and cried, and then someone touched me, "Who did it? Tell us."

Even my brother, who hated me, who always told me "to go away," and "don't talk to me," was speaking in a kind way to me. And then somehow, I was in the arms of the boy I secretly loved, and he was holding me and kissing the top of my head. And then because I didn't know the difference between love and attraction, I told them the name of the boy who had hurt me, and they knew his older brother and then they were gone to find the boy, to make him pay. Which had its own set of consequences.

. . .

Later, when my mother and Aunt Billie came home, they told me how it was my fault for riding my bike in alleyways and wearing short shorts and little halter tops, and how it didn't matter what everyone else wore or did. I was from a good family and we, our family, didn't dress like that to attract attention to our bodies.

This is how girls get raped, and their lives ruined, and they always bring it on themselves, because men are nothing but animals and it's up to women to protect not only themselves, but also the men from themselves. I got punished and forbidden to ride my bike for a week or go to the shopping center.

"Didn't I realize how this inconvenienced everyone else? I should go to the Catholic school, after all, so the nuns could teach me how to dress and comport myself properly." And that is how I got to go to the Catholic school.

On the first day, I walked to school with Clay, who was starting first grade. I took him to his class and then walked to mine. As I entered, the teacher, a tall, strict looking nun I had never seen before, pointed to my desk at the very back of the room. When I asked if my mother had told her about my hearing loss, she put a finger to her closed lips, signifying silence, and pointed toward my desk at the end of the aisle.

As I walked toward my desk, there he was, the fat boy with a pimple face and flat top, sitting in the middle of the same aisle and staring at me with a mean, knowing look. I was filled with a jolt of the shame I had carried since the alleyway incident and with a new fear.

He would tell. The boy would tell people I was a whore and people would believe him.

I knew I was powerless to stop him, and that no one would believe me. I realized I really was a horny girl. That I did want to kiss and be touched, but not by him.

As I walked up the aisle, I knew he would be seen as the tempted one and I would be seen as the temptress. I felt powerless to speak in my own defense, and the injustice of that imposed silence was overwhelming.

As the days wore on, I was proven correct. The Sister, who was both the Principal and my teacher, loved that boy. He was her pet; she couldn't do enough to help him overcome the effects of his public education that had not taught catechism or how to diagram a sentence.

The boy at recess was always with the other boys, laughing and pointing at me, telling them who knew what? And the Sister, Principal, Teacher who loved the boy, hated me. I started making Fs in every subject.

Within six weeks, I had to face up to the fact there was no salvation for me in the Catholic world. In the mind of that Sister, I was a failure and a sinner. I hated her for not recognizing the injustice and for not realizing the boy was a liar and the one at fault. And I couldn't say anything because, like my mother said, it was always the woman's fault.

I had to do the unthinkable, face the music, go to my mother, and tell her I had to switch back to public school where I had done so well and been happy. That is, until I had become filled with the Holy Spirit at Confirmation and entered a state of grace and been fooled into the notion I could be accepted by the nuns and students at the Catholic school.

Mother wanted to know, "Why?" I couldn't tell her about the boy. That was dangerous. Then I would have to hear again how it was all, "Your own fault. You brought it on yourself."

What mother said was, "Fine thing! Your brother is in first grade there, and now you want to leave. Who will bring him to school in the morning and pick him up after? They are in opposite directions." And if as I suggested, I bring him to Encanto Elementary, next door to Clarendon Middle School and if he didn't do well with the change, "It would be my fault that my little brother fails in school and never does well in life."

I persevered through a whole new level of guilt and fear.

Finally, Mother agreed to the switch for both of us. I never knew why. She died before I was old enough and free enough to ask her.

Perhaps, I reasoned, it was just the savings. Catholic school tuition was much cheaper in 1954 than now, but it was still a burden on our limited income. She knew what was going on. She knew things we did in which she didn't interfere. Was it because it just was not worth the effort it would have taken to bring into consciousness?

As for the blame I carried in regard to Vicki, forty years later I would find her thanks to one of those lists they put out on the internet.

We spent hours over lunch talking about our adolescent friendship and how unhappy we both were and that neither of us had real friends except for each other.

I discovered her family's move was very sudden and while she didn't feel guilty, she was sorry for not saying goodbye. She was also sorry for my guilt, and reassured me that she didn't remember me ever acting or being mean.

That long lunch helped me understand the misconceptions of memory of that long ago friendship and the power of that moment in time when she reached out to me. I didn't realize we shared the same deep loneliness.

I think about how we transcended our deep hurt into the simple games little girls played and the extraordinary skills we developed as we jumped rope and hopped on one leg. I think too about the joy in being able to pick up all the sticks which meant a double win of strategy when we gave up our own desire to beat the other, and figured out how to collaborate so that together, we beat the sticks.

CHAPTER 15
Trying On Bad

[1954]

I celebrated my release from Catholic school over a cherry coke float at a soda fountain near the school.

It was the set up for my first meeting with the biggest tramp in either school. Her name was Mary Ann. She had gone to Catholic school until she got expelled for doing something so bad; she ended up in reform school. She even had reform school tattoos on her ankles and wrists, made by cutting herself with a razor blade and pouring indelible ink into the bloody scars and adding more till the bleeding stopped.

It was rumored she had gone all the way with not one, but many boys and had been raped more than once.

I had never been near her or spoken to her. She was taboo. No self-respecting girl would speak to her. But by this time, I had not an ounce of self-respect left, so she was like fly paper, like sugar coating on a bitter pill that had to be swallowed. She was like forbidden candy during Lent beckoning to sweet-loving children. And she was also the most attractive girl I had ever heard of or thought to know. I was thrilled when she spoke to me and asked me to go to her house.

She lived in a small, two-bedroom frame house on the far side of the Middle School.

Mary Ann had her very own portable 45 Record Player. Her record collection included Bill Hailey and the Comets, Johnny Ray, Nat King Cole, Frank Sinatra, Bing Crosby, the Andrew Sisters, *Restless Wind, Rock Around the Clock*, Tennessee Ernie Ford, Rosemary Clooney singing *Mr. Sandman*, a new singer named Elvis Presley.

One day, Mary Ann and I skipped school to go to her house and listen to records.

Later, we walked around the streets and let a group of big boys from the senior high school, who had bad reputations, pick us up. They had a car, and we got in. Two of the boys, brothers, recognized me as being the daughter of a friend of their mother. They threatened to tell their mother if I ever did such a thing again. Even the bad boys recognized I was becoming a terribly bad girl. They didn't want me.

I felt so ugly, so unsexy, and yet my hormones were raging, forcing me to focus my attention down there where there was this huge void that longed to be filled. I kept trying to imagine what the sex act itself would look like because I was feeling things that were as forbidden to feel as to act on. Worse really, because it was a secret sin if it was in your head or, in my case, my vagina. It was a word I was not allowed to say, much less touch. My mind and vagina were now firmly fused and found wanton.

The first eighth-grade school dance of 1954 was approaching, and Mary Ann hatched a plan. We would each tell our mothers we were spending the night at the other's house, leave the dance, and pick up some boys.

I was terrified of lying to my mother, or rather, of getting caught. By then, I lied every day out of habit as well as survival. I genuinely loved my teachers at Clarendon, particularly after they greeted me so warmly on my return from three weeks at the Catholic school. But I was more afraid of disappointing my new friend than any loyalty I might have for my teachers. I would have gone to hell with her, and I almost did.

We snuck out, half an hour before the dance ended. It would have been wiser to wait till the dance was over.

We walked half a mile to a drug store far away from our neighborhoods. Sure, enough there were two high school boys whom I didn't recognize as being part of my brother's ROTC Unit or the sons of any of my mother's friends.

We flirted and soon we were walking back to one of the one of the boy's houses, which was a small apartment where he lived alone with his mother. She worked at night, which meant we had the sofa to ourselves for several hours.

I discovered the sweetness of French kissing and having a boy touch my breasts and rub between my legs with his hand. At some point in the night, Mary Ann and I walked back to her house and crawled into her bedroom window.

In the morning, her mother asked where we had been. "We were here all night." Mary Ann said but her mother just stared at us.

A little while later, my mother appeared. She took me home without a word and marched me straight into the bathroom where I had to take off my clothes, kneel and hold on to the toilet while she whipped me with a belt, me yelling in pain and shame, she yelling in anger, relief and disgust for the shame I had brought on myself and on her. Also for the terror I had put her through and the delight she was taking in being able to punish me.

But it would be the last time she would ever take a belt to me. She knew she had lost the battle of my remaining innocence. We both knew it was time for me to grow up.

. . .

Mary Ann and I had been missed from the dance. Our mothers were notified of our departure.

Mary Ann was expelled and sent back to reform school. She was out on probation for who knows what.

My mother and my favorite teacher forbade me from attending any school dances for the rest of the year. I knew my behavior made it possible for the terrible boy at the Catholic school to say anything he wanted about me. I knew I had been bad. I didn't want it to be that way. I wanted to be a good girl.

I spent the next several weeks being as good as good could be. In the back of my mind I thought about why Mary Ann had to go to reform school. She didn't corrupt me, and she certainly didn't do anything worse than me. I felt shame but I came to understand that what brought on the same was what others said or believed about me and not what I did.

A strange thing happened after the incident with Mary Ann.

The most popular girls in the school befriended me. They asked me to their parties, and we walked to school in the morning and home in the afternoons. I felt like I belonged and was forgiven and was magically popular.

First, Mary Ann the tramp and now the popular girls were my best friends. I do not remember what precipitated it, but one spring day on the way home from school, the popular girls told me that the only reason they were my friends was that Mr. Ralston asked them to be nice to me.

No one could be friends with someone like me. Nothing was right with me. My hair was always a mess; I had to sneak lipstick when everyone else could wear mascara and Max Factor makeup. And my clothes were embarrassing.

It was true. I wore dresses I made or were my mother and Aunt Billie's cast-offs. I had tried to make a hoop skirt with a bent clothes hanger. But I had to be careful when I sat or it popped up, exposing my bare legs and more.

And there was the crinoline for which I had gathered yards of net material onto elastic. Then, to make it stiff, I soaked it in sugar water in the bathtub. When it got hot or sat too long, it would stick to me.

I also had to be extra careful of spiders and scorpions nesting in it. Every morning, I would have to check and double check and shake it to make sure the bugs and insects were gone. I had hoped no one would notice any of these shortcomings.

The popular girls' revelation was hurtful and confirmed once more how out of place I was.

But this time I got angry. I was mad at those snotty girls who had fathers who loved them and mothers who took them shopping and let them pick out anything they wanted. I was mad at my teacher for asking people to be nice to me because it hurt so much when they weren't nice.

The next day at school, I got into a fight with some boy who was making fun of me and teasing. I started cursing right in the middle of class and tore into him with both fists flying and me crying.

Mr. Ralston made us both stay and fussed at the boy for teasing, and me for acting in such a violent, un-lady-like manner. But I had his attention. He excused the boy and asked me what happened to make me so angry?

"Did you ask those girls to be nice to me?"

I could tell he did, his eyes went all funny and his face twitched.

"What happened? Did you have a fight?"

"I thought they liked me. I thought I was a part of the popular group. They were so beautiful. I thought I was like them. They told me how awful I am, that I could never be one of them and they were tired of trying to help me. That they only took me in to please you and because they felt sorry for me."

"I'm so sorry. I did ask them. I was trying to make you feel better."

"And now I can't even go to my graduation dance, and everyone is laughing at me."

"Why can't you go to the graduation dance?"

"Because you told me I couldn't. You said I couldn't go to any more dances."

"Not for the full year. Just till after Christmas. I wanted to make sure you got Mary Ann out of your system. I don't know why I didn't warn you. I knew what a bad influence she could be." Mr. Ralston sat down on a desk, so he was level with me.

"What happened? Why did you leave the Catholic school? I don't even know why you went there."

And then I told him what happened during the summer and how it went at the Catholic school and how my only friend, Vicky, left, and how she was Jewish, how she was mad when I went to St. Michael's and became all religious and I was mean to her and feeling superior because I had Jesus and she didn't and how her family were the nicest people in the world, and if they had stayed none of this would have happened, and now my mother would never trust me and everybody knew I was bad and I was ruined.

By now, I was crying so hard my body was shaking, and the words were coming out in big blurbs like someone swimming and talking at the same time.

Mr. Ralston took me into his arms and held me and rocked me and cooed. Then I really cried because it felt like when the boy and I had sat on his mama's sofa French kissing and touching and holding on for dear life. It felt like my big brother reaching for me under the bed and his ROTC friend holding me. It felt so good to be held and rocked and cooed and to feel so safe and warm as though I was a valuable girl. To not feel like an ugly nerd with hair that stuck out every which way because my Aunt Billie cut it to save money, and I wore my mother's hand-me-downs and badly made skirts and outfits I worked so hard on but never turned out right.

. . .

I went to my grade school graduation wearing my mother's white dress. On my feet, I wore my first pair of French heels bought just for me. I had on lipstick and mascara and I felt pretty.

At the dance, none of the boys asked me to dance and none of the girls talked to me.

It hurt but it didn't really matter because I knew that somehow; I had grown up over the past year, and without any evidence to prove it, I knew that high school would be different and that I really was a good girl.

How I knew it, I know not. All I knew was that at the dance, I survived the snubs of the other kids, and I knew that a whole new world was opening for me, even if I didn't yet know what that world was.

Things did change after I entered my freshman year of high school.

The most important thing was that the Salk vaccine was made available throughout the country. We all lined up in the gymnasium for our shot. I remember how relieved and excited I was. But the excitement was dampened a bit by the kids and teachers who walked with iron braces on their legs.

One of my friends had spent the whole of eighth grade in a hospital being treated and learning to walk again with the heavy braces on her legs. She was bitter and angry that the vaccine was too late to help her. I avoided her because I really didn't know what to say.

That year there was one other factor I had to contend with when I had spent the early part of that same summer on bed rest because the doctors diagnosed me with a mild case of Polio.

I felt survivor's guilt because I had only been affected by a short-term bout of the disease.

Many years later, I noticed my left leg was becoming increasingly smaller and weaker than my right leg. In my early seventies, to walk safely I had to rely on a cane. But I had also damaged the same ankle several times over the years without ever properly fixing it. Part of it due to a lack of money in my younger years and part due to not wanting to miss a march or a visit to my grandchildren in my later years.

I made friends with new kids who had cars and whenever I could get away, we would drive out to the nearby mountains that held the ruins of an old Native American Civilization.

Music filled our world as we left the car motor running while we played the radio as loud as the car allowed. We would lay out on blankets brought from home and play eye games by squinting or crossing our eyes so we would be able to see the ghosts of Indians long dead walking up and down the ladders and layers of the ruins. I don't think sex as such played any part in that period.

Mama just wanted to get me out of town for a while so Julian and I received an early Christmas present in the form of two coach tickets on the Sunset Limited that began in Los Angeles and stopped in Phoenix taking us all the way to New Orleans.

She wanted Julian to walk around the Tulane campus and she also wanted me to see how nice it was in Louisiana, and as a special treat, we got to stop in Lake Charles to see our father.

I even got a new dark grey felt jumper and a soft yellow cotton sweater. Mama was working in better dresses at Goldwater's Department Store, where she got an employee discount. Her lungs seemed to be all better, even if she was still too thin.

The train from Los Angeles was loaded with colored families traveling home to the South. I had not seen so many Black people since leaving Covington.

I loved the sound of their dialects and the variance of dark shades of their skin. I had not forgotten Ruby and Betty. I sat with these new families instead of my brother, who would check on me from time to time.

Mama had fixed fried chicken and potato salad for us to eat on the train. She knew the salad would be good the first day and there was enough to share with the families I sat with who brought their own food to share.

Brother made me sleep in the seat next to him that night. But in the morning, all my new friends were gone. Julian explained that when we hit the Texas border, the trains became segregated, and all the colored families had to move to the back of the train.

Outraged, I walked all the way back to see the sign that read "Colored only." The older women told me, "Child you must leave this car. You'll get us all in trouble." I argued, "No, we all have the same ticket. They can't make me leave."

But before long, the red-faced Conductor and Julian, looking more embarrassed than I had ever seen him arrived, and dragged me back where I belonged. I was in disbelief and when I tried to get Julian to explain it, he just said, "Be quiet. Don't make any more trouble for us."

Those words reminded me of when we were still young in Covington and one of the older country boys that sat in our desks every year after haying season taught me an unfamiliar word, "fuck."

When I asked him what it meant, the other farm boys started laughing. Shortly after that school yard incident, Julian and I were in the Covington High stadium watching a night game our father was umpiring. I asked Brother what the word fuck meant. "I can't tell you. It's a bad word. Just don't say it again." Thinking he was being mean, I stood up over him and shouted, "Fuck! Fuck! Fuck!' until a man further down the row came over and told me that it wasn't a nice word for a little girl, and he knew my daddy would be ashamed of me.

Later, when we arrived in Lake Charles, Julian told me that the meanness of the South did not leave just because we did. And he reminded me of all the other customs I would have to get used to.

I thought I could get people to change, but first, I would have to change some of the fearful part of me.

How did I know that? I realized what bothered me most was the casual acceptance of the disturbing southern customs that made everyone complicit in the making of the unacceptable, acceptable or at least not something anyone really wanted to speak up about or change because it was dangerous.

All those years ago, when I was only fourteen, I awakened to the fact that so many of our beliefs and actions are a response to a rule of terror that has permeated all our lives and the lives of our ancestors. The addition of train cars and the movement of people became a metaphor for all the ways in which we willingly cast others into hell so that we can live in the safety of being acceptable.

As soon as Julian graduated from high school in 1956, Mama and Aunt Billie began preparations to move us back to New Orleans.

They had already sold the house and the Studebaker and bought an old station wagon with real wood trim on the outside panels. We planned to head north and visit the Grand Canyon since none of us had made it that far north during our five years in Arizona.

The movers came and the car was packed with everything we would need before we could find an apartment in New Orleans.

Billie was driving us when she lost the ability to shift or slow down the car. This happened at the top of a mountain that led down into Oak Creek Canyon. Without any braking ability, all she could do was steer her way down the mountain with mother screaming the whole time.

"Billie, slow down!"

"I can't Winnie, it won't brake!"

"Oh my God, we're all going to die."

"Shut up, Winnie, and let me drive."

Then our Aunt Billie prayed aloud, which was truly terrifying since it meant she didn't trust her driving ability as much as we did. But despite her fear, she steered that behemoth station wagon down the mountain where it safely rolled to a stop in the town of Sedona, which in 1956 had a small travel court, a post office, grocery store and gas pump.

There was also a mechanic shop. The old German mechanic discovered the problem lay not with the brakes but the differential gear. He sent off for a used one that might fit the car. That is how we got to spend a week in Oak Creek Canyon because every day the mail arrived with the wrong size part to fix our car.

CHAPTER 16
Return to the South

[1956 - 1959]

Mama and Aunt Billie were home, where the world was perfect for keeping a woman's skin young forever.

Their faces were always red and wet with sweat and heat, which Mama explained was a Southern Lady's glow.

Our black suede shoes had to be kept in old, torn nylon stockings to keep the mildew off them. Really! The stockings turned green with mold in the un-air-conditioned air.

And of course, home meant the iced tea was sweet, and you could find good people from old families and colored people who knew their place and kept it. Where ladies dressed up and wore white gloves spring and summer to Canal Street and soft, black leather gloves in the fall and winter.

I hated New Orleans. All I did was sweat and try to find respite from the heat. There was no air conditioning in our homes or schools. Open windows and fans were all we had.

And there were huge roaches that were fearless and could fly with the precision and speed of a British Spitfire. Not to mention the little ones that Mama said carried germs, but no amount of cleaning and killing could eradicate them. They took over our dresser drawers and kitchen cabinets. I was left longing for the scorpions and large spiders of Arizona, along with the dry heat of the desert that evaporated my sweat before my hair went all soggy.

After arriving, we stayed with Aunt Ellen and Uncle LC until Mama and Billie found an apartment.

Aunt Ellen, who could sew, made a new dress that fit me for school, and I helped watch the children. But my cousins were uncomfortable having all of us invade their space, not that I could blame them.

And there was a new cousin, a little boy named Lud, who became my favorite because of his sweet disposition.

An older girl who lived next door to Aunt Ellen showed me how to get around by streetcar and bus. Seven cents got you a ride and a transfer to move around the city. Canal Street became my playground as I discovered all the beautiful movie theaters.

That first year, I auditioned at Gallery Circle Theatre in the French Quarter and got a role in the newly released Broadway play *Ms. McThing*, written by Mary Chase, a successful woman playwright who was most famous for her play Harvey.

Theater became my passion. For the next three years, I showed up for every play the company produced. I was a pest, but there was no way to get rid of me except to call the police and get a restraining order. I learned about props and set design and costumes. I rode the streetcar from our apartment on Louisiana Avenue near St. Charles and walked the seven blocks through the quarter to the theatre and was never afraid. Someone would usually drive me home after the performances or at least make sure I got onto the streetcar.

Theatre saved my life or at least gave me a place where I was surrounded by adults who were not held back by the taboos of the time.

I got to meet gay men who, on one starry night helped calm me down after an altercation with a young man high on drugs who had pushed me and tried to steal my purse.

After the police arrived to collect the evidence about my stolen purse, which was never to be seen again, several of the guys loaded me into their convertible. One of them was the sweetest as he held me in his arms while kissing me. When I declared my love the driver stopped the car and the young men told me all kinds of important things about sex that no on had ever told me, not even in my sex education classes at Encanto.

I should have been mortified. But they were kind, and I knew they were right about what they were sharing with me.

They said sex was a gift to comfort, to have fun, to treasure, but never to allow anyone to hurt me.

They cautioned me not to mistake lust for love and to be careful not to give my body away too easily. I remember they said I had the most beautiful smile. As as they said it how I could hear Mama's words instructing me not to smile so much and to cover my buck teeth with my lips. Those men made me feel beautiful.

Years later, I would respond to the terrible AIDS epidemic that killed so many gay men in the '80s and '90s by becoming a patient care volunteer in Houston's first AIDS hospice.

Interestingly, the common denominator of the volunteers was Tuberculosis. All of us, both paid staff and doctors plus volunteers, had a family member who had the disease.

Gay or straight we all knew the hurt of discrimination and the fear of isolation, as we witnessed that same ugly head rise again even as young children who picked up the HIV virus from blood transfusions were denied the use of chlorinated community swimming pools and students in some schools were denied a seat in a classroom or had to sit isolated from the other students.

So great was the fear some funeral homes refused to prepare bodies for burial and some churches refused funeral services to the families of brothers, sons and fathers who died not just in sin, but from a contagious disease.

. . .

Later I would become a spiritual director in a retreat center founded by the Sisters of the Cenacle and on several occasions, I was able to help mothers understand their sons were still their sons and could have good lives and bring much joy to their families.

In my late sixties, I taught storytelling in an inner-city university with the goal of using stories as a way to create empathy. I cannot imagine a life without books and movies or music and art. I had found my voice, and I wanted to hear the voices of my students.

I hated my new school in New Orleans and managed to make enemies on my first day when I told a boy who was ogling me that I had seen him on the streetcar that morning. I asked him if it was fair for him to tell an older Black woman in a white maid's uniform to give up her seat for him, thus causing her to have to stand behind the sign that read *white only* on one side and *colored only* on the other. I noticed he was large and heavy. Turned out he was a guard on the football team. He stared down at me with a mean and threatening face and shouted for all to hear, "Hey, we got us a nigga lover!"

What was I thinking? I still have trouble letting things rest. I wonder now if my reaction to the rules of segregated seating on the city buses and street cars would have been so strong if I had not experienced the adding of segregated cars on our trip by train to Louisiana in the winter of 1954?

It was egregious but so was asking or rudely telling a person of color to move to the back of public transportation.

Everyone paid the same fare. It was such a graphic experience of cruelty and disdain of the other that it broadened my ability to recognize hatred that is disguised as just the way it is by polite society.

It has made me a lousy dinner guest as I hurt people's feelings without meaning to, by merely questioning their lifelong assumptions that they made their way in life without help from anyone and then finish that statement with the question of "why can't blacks do the same?" When, I mention there may be certain privileges, we gain by virtue of our skin color it is taken as a personal assault. I didn't have the vocabulary to articulate any of that in high school. Like most people, I just had to survive.

Mama had this unrealistic idea that I would become popular with the girls from *good* families. I found the girls from those supposed *good* families to be closed off, at least from me. And looking back on it, the girls from the families she wanted me to meet and cultivate as friends did not go to public schools.

Those girls went to private school. There wasn't money for me. Julian was at Tulane and since he was a boy and needed to make a profession for himself, it was up to me to make my way and eventually find an acceptable husband.

None of that was said. It was implied. Julian might bake a cake, but I cleaned up his mess. I was being prepared for marriage, and I had no good role models. It's interesting to note that after Julian's marriage he took over washing dishes and as his wife withdrew from life, he became the shopper.

The popular girls at my new school were even less interested in me than the mean girls I encountered in eighth grade. They obviously didn't recognize my good background. I didn't even have a clue as to what made us such a good family. Mama never taught me the skill of moving into a new group or feeling like I belonged because after her divorce she no longer belonged, and we had to move from a lovely small town where she had lived for most of her life and there was a built-in community of friends.

Mama had something I didn't develop for a long time and never. She was haughty. She could move with assurance into any of *her* approved societies. The difference is I don't have to approve of any one group.

My natural extroversion made it possible for me to like being a part of a crowd, but I was much more at home with one or two friends. The whole time I was in high school, I never felt like I had a friend except for a nice girl named Margie whose working-class family mother, disapproved. And like Vicky, she wasn't welcome in the apartment I shared with my brothers and my mother and aunt, which on reflection might have had more to do with space and privacy than prejudice.

Margie was my school friend and after-school friend. I was welcome at her home and on day trips with her parents to visit her mother's family. I wanted to integrate, not segregate.

East Louisiana was dotted with small farms where Margie's country cousins lived.

We always arrived in time for the midday meal served from a long table filled with bowls of vegetables and ribs and fried chicken and pork chops. The girl cousins were all healthy beautiful girls whose tans and well-developed bodies came because of demanding work and play with their brothers and cousins. I've often wondered what became of those girls.

Did they go to college and leave the farms behind and find careers or did they stay and work and have babies until their beautiful bodies broke down because of the same work that made them so strong and beautiful in youth?

Were they abused or made to feel less than, or were they loved and cherished?

Were they forced to sell the land and beauty they knew in youth?

Did they become bitter old women, or did they feel blessed by what they had accomplished even as it all disappeared?

Did they, like so many of us old women who cooked three meals a day for a lifetime take all the experiences good and bad and deep life abiding emotions and make them all into a list of ingredients for a large gumbo or pot of soup seasoned with bits of remembered sunrises and sunsets? Or for shadow moons and eclipses and full moons that light the way into ourselves, even after our menses stopped and to this day remain our internal clocks?

Margie and I both sang in the girls' chorus and ushered at the New Orleans Symphony and Opera Company.

I could not sing Amen by myself but in a group I did okay.

Our chorus teacher would loan all her students large bound books that contained the scores for music we would listen to and taught us to follow the melody line that the violins played. That way we had a visual image of what we were hearing by seeing where the different instruments called into the piece countering the melody with horns, drums, and clatter, and waking our souls to the beauty of the music.

We made friends with two boys who were artistically inclined, and the four of us had lunch together every day on a street near our school that had a small boulevard. That way we could smoke and drink soft drinks that we bought at the snack shop near the school.

I never bothered to make lunch, so I usually bought a bag of peanuts. By the time I graduated high school I weighed less than a hundred pounds which was not a lot on my 5-foot frame, and my health was paying for it.

In my junior year, I took American History with a woman, a fine teacher, who thought I had the ability to be a good debater. I did not believe her, but she wanted one or two strong debaters to speak on behalf of the admittance of Red China to the United Nations.

The only thing I knew about the topic was that Mama was against it. I slowly raised my hand when no one else did. A couple of hours in the public library and I realized I had enough facts to make a winning argument. I did not believe for a minute I would win the debate, but when I faced my opponents with facts to their overly emotional arguments, I easily won.

But the win against three boys added a new epithet to my presence in the hallways and the cafeteria, where my lunch group was forced to eat during thunderstorms.

"Hey, this girl is a communist!"

Early in my senior year, I missed the first weeks of school. I had emergency exploratory surgery. The surgeon also removed my appendix, leaving me with a long scar down the right side of my abdomen.

One warm fall afternoon after getting on the Freret Street bus that stopped across Nashville Avenue from the school, I found two young Black women staging a sit-in protest on the bus. I was the first one on and the kids forced me toward the back of the bus before they realized what was happening.

People were yelling at the two young women, and the bus driver was yelling at everyone.

Trapped and exhausted, I sat a few rows behind the two protesters. The bus erupted. Kids stood over me, shouting over and over, the same ugly epitaphs. Those two girls didn't deserve this outrage, and neither did I.

I realized for the first time I was more connected to African Americans than to most of the White adults and kids I had met since coming back to the South.

Then the police came to take the two protesters off the bus, and I assume to the police station. I made the connection between my short-lived friendship with Mary Ann in Phoenix when we both skipped out of the dance and she was sent back to reform school for the same offense as me and now two black girls were going off to jail and the police left me who broke the same rule, going home, with kids still muttering about my strange affections under their breath.

By this time, my anger over the name calling I was subjected to had built to a dangerous level. That same semester I was kicked out of my journalism class for making the teacher and students angry over my handling of my first assignment to draft a sports article for the school newspaper.

Instead of writing about the game itself which we lost, I wrote about the fashions of the game goers and the pitiful cheerleader costumes which consisted of long, full, circular skirts that hindered acrobatic movement and were so old and worn even the beautiful girls on the squad looked drab.

Another paragraph described the peanut salesman at the games called Evolution and tied it to our biology teacher's refusal to teach about Darwin or evolution. Could I have been that smart then? Maybe.

But not so brave as to take on the biology teacher I liked despite her rejection of science. I have no idea if I was kicked out for not writing about the game or if they didn't like what I did write because I received no feedback and I did not demand any.

A year later my future husband told me that Evolution got his name because he acted like a monkey, climbing the chain-link fences and pounding on his chest like an ape. It was an example of performance art that made the peanut salesman a lot of money, which he needed to raise his many children.

I also signed up for a new class in drama. Our new teacher was casting a play using senior students. I was cast as the maid. She explained I was absent so much she dared not cast me in a lead role.

As I remember the dialogue showed the maid to be a stereotypical Black character. I am sure that is how I played her. On the day of the performance, I covered my body and face with black make-up without discussing it with our teacher. In my ignorance I did not put a layer of cold cream on first, so after the performance the make-up stayed on my body like a second skin.

I tried getting it off with soap and paper towels with little success. Since it was exam week, I walked the halls showing my true colors or, more likely, giving my fellow students a walking *fuck you* sign. Not the principal or any of my teachers said a word. No one suggested I use the available showers in the gym. I did hear an occasional comment from fellow students, "You are one crazy girl."

The hard part was riding the bus home and getting that make-up off before Mama or Aunt Billie got home from work. I used a whole bottle of cold cream. When they asked, I confessed to breaking it accidentally. I realized even back then it was a silly thing to do, there was no way to feel like I was Black.

I was white and I hated segregation and at the same time I was fearful of the very people I was segregated from. That fear was so ingrained that losing the fear would take a long while.

In the spring of my senior year, my mother showed me a notice in the *Times Picayune* for a group that was holding auditions at the Jung Hotel for Oscar Wilde's play, "The Matchmaker." Most of the group knew each other from their student days at Loyola University.

I caught the streetcar and read a love scene with a handsome, young man named Ted. He was over six feet tall, and wore his dark hair in a pompadour. He had just returned to New Orleans after several years at Notre Dame, where he dropped out of school to work as a disc jockey for a classical station to wait for the draft. He had just finished a two-year hitch in the army.

I got the smaller part of the shopgirl but the rehearsals were difficult to get to without a car as they were held in a neighborhood called Metairie. Making the bus connections was hard so Ted agreed to pick me up at the bus stop by the cemeteries and drop me off there to catch my bus back home. The trouble was late at night, the buses did not run as regular as daytime so I might have to wait 20 or 30 minutes alone in the dark.

When Ted was chosen to direct the second play of the summer season, he cast me in the ingénue role in "My Three Angels."

He was seven years older, so I did not assume he had any romantic interest in me. Ted was intelligent but also kind to the actors he directed and in the way he treated everyone, but I was terribly shy around him.

At the last cast party of the summer we sat on the steps of a house in the French Quarter where our rehearsals had been and talked half the night away.

He told me he planned to begin law school in a few weeks. And I told him about my college plans.

At some point we kiss and all that hunger I had stuffed away returned, only now I was eighteen and finished with high school. I wanted to have sex.

Ted asked me out the next weekend and took me to dinner and a cocktail lounge. And then sitting in his dad's car at the seawall along Lake Ponchatrain, he asked me to marry him.

If I had been older, I would have realized he was on the rebound and wanted a young wife who he could boss around. But I told him I could not even imagine getting married yet. He was pushing me for an answer so I hedged and said if he were willing to wait a year we would see.

As soon as I got to college in a small town a couple of hours from New Orleans, I was cast in another play.

Between that and traveling home every weekend to be with Ted, my grades plummeted. So, I quit and went back home to find a job and to wait and see what developed with our engagement.

Besides, I knew there was not enough money for me to go to school and I had hoped my dad would help, but that never happened.

CHAPTER 17
Mama's Opus

[1959]

All that fall, Mama's nightly ritual began after dinner. Dressed in her bright green silk pajamas, she placed an unfiltered Pall Mall into her long black cigarette holder with the dragon painted on its side as she sat in her favorite overstuffed green chair, upholstered in several patterns of clashing fabric.

It was Mama's fault. To save money, she did not really have in the first place, she insisted the upholsterer order only half the amount of fabric he said was required. A wicked man, he followed her instructions to the letter and then pieced the shorter fabric with remnants on another fabric that merely blended. She did not pay him. And he didn't force the deal because, well, she was charming, and had a headache and it was a game she played to get at least part of what she wanted.

One little seed of memory, and I'm off in the maze that was my young self's impressions of the mystery I called Mama. Before she lit her cigarette, she picked up her yellow legal pad, the green ink fountain pen she favored, and folding her long legs up against her body, she finally spoke.

"I think I will work on the part where he dies." She stared off into space, the fountain pen held suspended over the page. "I don't think being shot by the sheriff was good enough for your daddy, honey. Yes, I'll kill the bastard again."

A pause, and then the scariest thing of all came out of her mouth, "I've been thinking," as she smiled widely, showing her crooked teeth.

"...one of his accidents. Yes, that would be so much more appropriate." A puff of smoke rose in an upward spiral.

"A fiery accident."

Mama never bothered with a cigarette lighter because, as she told anyone who asked, "Too much bother and always needing something like a flint or lighter fluid."

She kept kitchen matches in little demitasse cups that had lost their saucers. She struck the matches on the underside of any available piece of furniture, filling the air with the smell of sulfur. And then surrounded by a ring of smoke, she continued speaking and began to write.

"John in a drunken stupor...no, a wild rage...I want him fully awake; he has to feel the flames, remember the cattle guard honey, how he would jump that thing before the bars were in place, do you remember?"

On these long evenings, I would be sitting in another mismatched chair, smoking a cigarette, my own book set aside. By the time I was a teenager, I had placed my parents in separate rooms inside my brain. Their divorce was my fault. For as long as I could remember, my daddy said he loved me better than Mama. But I knew I needed my mother more than I needed my father, and it was easier to keep my feelings for him locked up than make an enemy out of Mother.

I was seven years older than my little brother, Clay. A strange kid, he was always doing his homework or reading an encyclopedia for fun. And shortly after learning to read, he would study the words in our copy of Wester's Dictionary beginning at the letter A.

Clay was a baby when our daddy left. He did not remember Military Road or our father. In his entire life, he only met our father three times. It was not like he had an emotional attachment to him, but I never did know what Mama thought about her children hearing all her pent-up rage at our father and the rest of the male world. Did she ever consider the consequences of her words and actions?

While Mama was talking, Clay lay on the floor with an open book. He listened to the chapters of Mother's Opus with quiet disinterest. But I suspected he was not missing a word.

"Henry. No. John... why did I marry a man named Henry?" It was a rhetorical question, so Clay and I remained silent.

"In his rage, he missed the turn and hit one of the brick columns that gave grace to the entry of the modest country home that Rachel made elegant on the meager money John gave her every week after much begging on her part... Does that sound right, honey?"

"I think so, Mama. What happens next?"

"Well, I think I'll have the priest in the house having dinner with Rachel and the children. No, I don't think the children should be there," She put down the pad on the table while she began to smoke in earnest, as if the tobacco helped her think.

"...but I don't believe it would be proper for the priest to be there for dinner if Rachel is all alone." She paused.

"No, it's all right." She took up her pen and began to write.

"John promised to be home for dinner." She looked up, "I'll have to go back and work on this. Writing a novel is so hard, honey." Her attention was divided between explaining herself and the unfinished page.

"...you make one slight change...and it affects something else...it's like making a fancy French sauce. You have to make five sauces in order to make the one the recipe calls for... remind me to teach you someday."

She gave me her full attention as it got close to bedtime.

"Why don't we have some of that leftover chocolate cake,

honey? And you fix my coffee for me, OK? And I'll think my way through this."

I'd go to the kitchen to boil the milk for Mama's *café au lait*. It took a steady eye because just as the milk came to a full boil and was about to flow out of the pot, I had to pour in the left-over French-dripped coffee one of us had made in the morning. I turned the fire off and let the fat gather on the top of the coffee-colored milk, then skimmed it off with a spoon as I poured the milk into her cup. The steam made my face feel warm and moist. Then I walked with the cup to the table and stirred in a quarter of a sugar shell spoon of sugar. My nightly rituals were all part of my mother's needs.

By now, Clay had come in to help with the cake. There was always a cake, homemade, sweet with dark chocolate icing. We would serve our mother as she continued the marathon telling of the many deaths of our father, and we ate our bedtime treat, licking the clinging bits of chocolate icing off the tines of our forks.

The sweetness of the cake combined with the voice of our mother morphed into a lasting tableau of sound and taste as Mama continued her latest addition.

"Rachel and Fr. Richard were having a bourbon and water when the sound of the crash reached their ears. They ran to the door in time to see the explosion. John's screams could be heard over the roar of the fire as they rushed past the azaleas to the end of the driveway. Fr. Richard prayed the Our Father in Latin." Mama put down her pen and, taking a long draw on her cigarette, sighed, "Hmmm, this is the best yet. I'll copy the prayer out of my missal."

It was 1959. My brother, Julian, was in New York City, a Woodrow Wilson Scholar attending Columbia for his masters.

It was just our little brother Clay, me, and Mama now. Aunt Billie left us that year to finally try to find her own life. I wanted to do the same. Find my own life. By the end of the summer that year, I was engaged.

I had my own book to write. I didn't believe I could write it, though. I thought if I ever did, it would be a mystery, as in murder. In a way, I have, but not the kind of murder mystery I used to disconnect from the pain of childbirth, as I read Agatha Christie novels through my labors.

Instead, I drafted a book that brought me straight into the terror of finding out the truth behind the beautiful faces and memories of Mama and her sisters.

When I came home from college, late that fall, Aunt Billie took me aside and said she was moving out and finding her own apartment. She and Mama had been fighting over money and everything else for the last year. Mama would write a check but never enter it into the check book, leaving Billie to explode when she checked the balance with the bank or got a notice that a check had bounced.

She hoped Mama would change, but of course my mother just passed her inability to budget on to me. So, every night after work, I would get a call from my mother to please pick up some groceries for dinner that night. I was trying to save money for setting up my own house but she poopooed that, saying, "You'll get everything you need from wedding presents."

At first, she approved of Ted, until she discovered he came from the wrong Pfister family branch.

One branch included highly educated professionals, but Ted's branch was working class. His grandparents on both sides had immigrated. his father's from Germany and his mother's from Italy.

His father and three of his five brothers left school after eighth grade. His dad worked for the same company until his retirement fifty years later. All of Ted's cousins went to college and had careers. None of that mattered to my mother when she discovered his father had married an Italian. Her demeaning behavior was not lost on Teddy or his mother.

By late spring 1960, I knew Ted and I were going to marry and that I was ready.

We decided late August would be best. I wanted a simple wedding to be held at the Prytania Street Chapel. I had visions of a dotted Swiss dress and a bouquet of daisies. Mama had other ideas.

First, she moved us to a lovely apartment in a large house on the corner of St. Charles and Nashville Avenue. And we joined Holy Name Parish; the church affiliated with Loyola University. She insisted it would be valuable and that for the rest of my life, I could feel proud to say I was married in that church.

She was planning an uptown wedding on the cheap. Holy Name was on the campus of Loyola University, and even though Ted was both a graduate and attending its Law School, you had to live in the Parish to become a member.

Luckily, in high school I worked on Saturdays in the bridal department of Krieger's Department Store on Canal Street where mother sold Better Dresses. The buyer who was married to the dental surgeon that removed my wisdom teeth, one of the things I did on my dime before my marriage, sold me a lovely Bianchi dress that was a size ten for the grand price of $35.

It was one of the sample dresses that brides tried on to see how the style looked on them. All through high school, the alterations from a size 10 to whatever I wore would not have worked. But working and eating lunch or breakfast and of course Sundays at my future Mother-in-law's put some meat on my bones. I was now a size eight and the biggest expense was the alterations at forty dollars.

Things between Ted and my mother became more and more

distant. And then she committed a grave error. She did not include his grandmother, Angelina Profumo Cusimano, in the invitation list to my only wedding shower.

When my mother-in-law told me, I thought it was a mistake. But when I asked Mama, she told me she would have been embarrassed to have her friends hear the old lady's heavy accent. I think for the first time I realized how embarrassed I was by my mother's prejudices and how ashamed I felt for not confronting them.

My father was not invited, but he sent me a check for $500 which I turned over to Mama for the reception. Part of my small savings paid for Julian's morning suit and my maid of honor and only attendant, Beth's aqua dress and the shoe dye. In the 1960s no wedding was complete without matching shoes for the attendants. I also chose a bouquet of gardenias and a smaller one for Beth.

The night before the wedding, Mama made a long white veil that was held together with artificial orange blossoms. She had a talent for putting things together at the last moment and making them work. Then the day before the wedding, while I was at the beauty parlor getting my hair and nails done, mother and her sisters were at Aunt Ellen's making small canapés and sandwiches.

The reception was a home affair for only fifty of the invited guests. Mother chose the apartment for that purpose. It had a large crescent-shaped room filled with shaded light due to the porte-cochere that was part of our apartment. I threw my corsage into a crowd of cousins and my Maid of Honor from the wrap-around porch that was supported by Corinthian columns.

My cousin, a photographer for the Times Picayune took all the photos and gave us of an album of engagement and wedding photos.

For years, I thought this was really Mama's wedding. Not a

dime was spent on a towel or a sheet for my trousseau. It all went to a wedding I didn't think I wanted or needed.

Only now do I love looking at the joy on my face in the old wedding album when my cousin gave me neat handwritten notes on who gave us what so I could mention the gifts in the many thank you notes I carefully wrote in the first days of marriage.

We spent our honeymoon in a new hotel near downtown.

At my shower I had gotten several of the flimsy little tops and shorts lingerie. They were all varying shades of pink. Not my favorite color, but I looked adorable. I packed them, but I never put them on until we got home from our short trip. I discovered as soon as I undressed that I loved being naked. I felt comfortable with my body and Ted's. He had a heavy beard and was shaving in the bathroom when I walked in, sat on the toilet and took a pee. He looked at me with surprise.

"Oh thank God, you're not shy and want to dress and undress in the closet."

"Nope, we're married."

Later in bed, both of us sweaty despite the air conditioning, I looked at him and asked, "Why is this not a sin today but was yesterday?"

"Because that's what the church teaches. I can't believe you told the priest we had sex."

"I can't believe you lied."

The priest who married us required an interview with us one at a time several weeks before the wedding. He asked if I had ever had intercourse? And as he was a priest, I answered truthfully without naming Teddy.

"So, it's fine to lie to a priest?"

Ted looked at me like I was stupid. "It was none of his business."

I would find his mother more particular on the subject of sex inside of marriage. But this was our honeymoon, and we finally went out for dinner at a nearby Italian Restaurant on Carrolton Avenue.

Back at the hotel, we had sex one more time, and he was down for the count. Thinking we would sit up and watch movies together, I bought a bag of popcorn at a nearby movie house. So, I was up for the night and watched David Copperfield on television.

I was drinking champagne, eating popcorn and thinking about having sex with my husband. I had a thought and found his underwear and the dress shirt he wore that night and put them on so I could maybe feel what he felt. I sat up for a few more hours, thinking about how to bring our shared experience alive inside of me.

Ted and I had a rocky start in the beginning. He had found us an apartment that was very small. Like a bedroom, kitchen and small entryway where his desk and a bookshelf fit. And a straight-back chair fit, but not another thing.

His choice was entirely about price rather than any consideration for comfort or space.

It was a distance to a bus line or a grocery. There were no corner stores. Since I didn't drive or ever need to, that alone was huge.

The bathroom had a small metal shower, toilet and sink. But my closet was a metal rod next to the shower. His suit hung in an armoire and his chest of drawers arrived filled to the gill with his clothes neatly folded and left no room for any of my belongings.

An only child he never thought of any of my needs, and he never learned the art of sharing. And his expectations of my daily role were a disaster.

Thinking back, it was funny, like a routine in a sitcom. But this was my life. I worked in an office while he studied and went to class. Then he worked at a television station from 5pm to 10pm.

He would arrive home after 10pm and want to eat a full dinner followed by sex. After a month I skipped work and went to his mother and grandmother.

All I had to say was, "The apartment...." In unison, these two marvelous women shouted, "We know. We have another apartment all picked out for you. Do you mind living close by?"

Until we could move, Ted's father picked me up after work and drove me to his house where I was fed and a dinner for Ted was placed in my hands before his father drove me back home.

Finally, Ted began to go to his mother's to eat before he went to work, and I went after work. We ultimately wound up living in a much nicer apartment thanks to his grandmother.

Ted huffed and puffed but all of us knew it was temporary.

His friends had all married right after graduation from college and were well established. My friends were in school. And while I was able to find my way into the lives of his friends and their wives, I lost touch with Margie.

All along, Ted was dictating his case summaries to me and we would discuss the law. Sometimes when it had to do with a woman's issue, I would read the case law and debate him from my point of view. And then I would sit with his exam study group and listen in as they discussed issues and law that might appear on the exam. Then during the course of the night, we would all get very drunk.

I married a brilliant man who was incredibly stupid, a lonely little boy who was terrified of failure. But he had an innate kindness, a keen sense of fair play that made up for all his mistaken ideas of how the world should work. As for me, well, I had a lot of growing up to do. The only difference between us was, I knew it and he still didn't have a clue.

Two of his professors took me under their wings. One introduced me to a great books discussion group.

I was shy at first, but I was encouraged to enter the discussion.

I remember the first book we read was "The Stranger." A novel by Albert Camus. I had never read anything like this book before. Except I had read the "The Day the Mountain Fell." I recognized the despair and the loss of hope as well as the determination of both the shepherd and the wife, as well as, the symbolism. And I also recognized myself.

There was one other redeeming quality that needs to be mentioned. That bookcase I mentioned in passing earlier. I read every book on those shelves.

Like Julian, Ted's first major had been English. While he had no science fiction, he did have a collection of American and English writers. I read all those books, even his philosophy and theology texts. And later, after our move back into the center of New Orleans, I caught buses and streetcars to the library where I would systematically read every novel or collection by a favorite author. I was becoming an educated woman on a variety of subjects.

CHAPTER 18
Mama (Part 1)

[1960 - 1965]

After I married, Mama moved herself and Clay into a roach infested apartment in a house on Music Street right off the streetcar line.

The living room was small and stacked with furniture until better times. She had left the department store and took a job as an assistant to the owner of an advertising firm that paid less than the department store but was more prestigious.

And sure enough she met a man. An older man, a lawyer who was a lifelong resident of Washington D.C. He would fly in and out of New Orleans frequently as he had long ago made connections with the family of his former wife who had died along with their only son from different kinds of Cancer.

As it turned out, his wife and her sister were distant cousins of my mother. However, when the sister introduced my mother to her brother-in-law, it was a match. Finally, my mother was being introduced into the society of the good people of New Orleans. As in, well-to-do attorneys with large Catholic families. And then she was engaged and left Clay with Ellen and L.C. who had also left New Orleans and moved to Covington shortly after our wedding.

In 1961, Mama married the elderly attorney who had a large home in Washington, D.C. but Mama believed in bullshit. Her new husband wanted a trophy wife, a woman who knew how to play the game. A woman who would follow his lead, agree with him, and not make scenes in front of his friends. And for God's sakes, who would open her legs when he had a need or want and not go on and on about the unfairness of the Church and then cut him off for fear of her immortal soul.

In July of of that year, Mama moved to Washington, D.C. and since Mama's new husband had connections, she went to the lectures at the Washington Press Corp.

While we were on different sides on everything political, mama filled her letters with the names and opinions of the reporters and editors she talked to about the world events of the sixties.

As time went by, she wrote about strange (to me) conspiracy theories. Even though she was sending Clay to Gonzaga, a Jesuit High School she hated the liberal teachings of those men and the changes of the Vatican II, which in her view was destroying the Church.

Late in the summer after Mama left New Orleans, she and I began writing weekly letters to each other. But her letters sounded like another person, like a character in a novel.

Could mine have sounded the same to her? Our letter writing was a form of journaling.

We were writing to ourselves or the selves we wanted to become. But she was in Washington, D.C. and I loved hearing about the gossip, and the stories about the people she met, and her assessments even if I did not agree with them because she was living in the heart of history.

I did not save all mama's letters, but amazingly I found about twenty partial and full letters that gave me a renewed sense of her adventures and obsessions. Even an invitation to the Kennedy White House for a luncheon with the First Lady.

But despite all that, we continued to fight some of the same old battles along with some new ones. Always a few steps forward followed by a few steps back.

At first, she and Bob seemed incredibly happy, but even early on the cracks began to show, mostly over money. Mama was cash poor and had to depend on her husband for the money to get all of us there for a visit, even to get Clay to Washington from Louisiana.

Our father was now responsible to send, only $75 a month for Clay, missing payments when he thought he could get by without paying. But Bob was a lawyer and not going to let him get by with it. Bob had his own methods for controlling mother's purse strings.

August 22, 1961

Jere dear – I can understand how Clay is more than ready to come up and Bob and I are looking forward to our loving son's arrival – Did make a reservation for Thursday and broke it because Julian said they would be here after the 25th, that is they would leave after the 25th – This morning I had a letter from him, stating that he was not sure if or when the girls (Julian's friends) would come up – Bob and I were so thrilled when he called the other night and said he was driving up with the girls and would bring Clay – We thought it was great and if it was safe for Julian, certainly safe for Clay – Also considered the fact that what it would cost for Clay to fly would pay for both and Julian's return trip – We *told him to ask the girls to stop over at least one nite and day to rest and were planning quite a house party – We even figured how all could have a bed!!!*

I am sure Julian can't afford such a trip now anyway and Bob was so happy he is coming – so if it's possible for Clay to come up that "away" see no reason why not –

I called Julian the other night cause he is the oldest—today I'm writing only you...

At the end of the long letter that must have been written over the course of several days, she writes:

P.S. Jere, I sent Julian the check so if he comes up and brings Clay he shall have the funds – if not he [can] go down and pick up the ticket for you-thanks for taking care of Clay – Love, Mom –

This wangling of money drove me crazy. At first, she's even having trouble getting Clay to Washington, as Bob *forgets* to write the check before he leaves for his office. She doesn't know how to confront him. She has spent her life being sneaky to get some of what she needs. Now that she has caught the golden ring, she is slow to realize the cost.

A short time later, after Clay's arrival, she writes about Bob's jealousy over the time she spends with Clay and the money he is spending on Clay's education and our father's lack of interest in his own son.

As I reread these letters, I can see how much pressure she is under. At first, she writes, "This marriage and love was truly made in heaven." She was surrounded by wealth, silver, China, and linens that have never been used, but she is still money poor as she contemplates returning wedding presents that are duplicates of things they already have. She knows full well if she is caught it will embarrass her new husband and she might lose his respect, but she is desperate for a few dollars of her own, something no one ever allowed her.

A letter to Clay:

Clay dear – guess what! Bob said we could have a dog – so when you come up, we shall pick it out. I'm so very happy and Bob is beside himself with joy – Washington is more beautiful than I dreamed possible at this time and much cooler. Ted [Bob's brother] just called – we are [going] to Church and lunch with him tomorrow – then the Williams? are having a party for us tomorrow evening alone – Have lunched with Bob each day at the Press Club. (Bob and I) have had so little time together with so many people each nite –
    This has been the most wonderful experience for both of us – We know now that it was made in heaven –

Later she writes concerning a trip planned for me to travel to Washington to see her and her new life.

P.S. By the way it was Bobs idea on your trip up however guess we shall have to wait his mentioning it – If you can think of some way to indicate you could or would with [out] mentioning what I revealed do so or just leave it alone until he does so – He is such a doll but says things and then forgets about it sometimes till later.

Things in my life were waking me up to how men react or try to control women, even apart from marriage.
    When I went to register to vote shortly after my twenty-first

birthday in 1962, I was turned down. The Jim Crow laws were used against white women as well as women and men of color.

I had to answer twenty-one questions on the Constitution and miscellaneous subjects. I was turned down because the last question was a trick. You had to give your age in years, months, weeks, and days. The registrar got to choose which day to count. It was a matter of going back the next day and using his formula. But it was inconvenient because of work. I passed.

I was now eligible to vote and the first thing I did was join the League of Women Voters who, as it happened, were in the process of coaching black women on how to pass the registration test.

The '60s were the most invigorating time of my life. I finally found myself fitting into the world around me, both socially and intellectually.

I was surrounded by people who were stimulating and did not make me feel stupid or socially unaccepted. Quite the opposite. Older women were reaching out to me, not only accepting what I thought about but what I believed. And low and behold they agreed with me or pointed out books that might be helpful for me to read. I was learning how to navigate the tricky world of politics, and most of all I was learning about my city, not just the French Quarter, uptown, and university areas, but the whole city.

I was also learning about the people, both Black and White. I was learning that we all sacrificed some part of our values and beliefs in order to stay safe. And how we all let ourselves down in ways that made us cringe.

I met Black Women who were light skinned and, when absolutely necessary, passed so that could find shelter for their families in segregated hotels. I learned about the small houses and large boarding houses and camps on the outskirts of New Orleans that sheltered Black musicians and singers and doctors because they weren't accepted in the segregated hotels. I was becoming aware and making decisions that frightened me based on what felt like the right thing to do. I also learned how to drive.

Not to mention I was pregnant during the last six years of the '60s. I gave birth to four babies and was awake for the first three. I celebrated every moment of birthing, as I prayed to the Blessed Mother to keep me safe, and allow me to withstand the pain of labor. I prayed to her about her labor with baby Jesus. And years later, I would read about some council or other of men deciding that Mary didn't have any birthing pains because she was blessed. And I thought, "Only men."

And even though I had inverted nipples, and it was difficult, I nursed the first three of my babies or at least fed them milk I pumped from my breasts. I loved my body and the bodies of my children. And Ted helped me as much as he could. Every night, we sang, "On Top of Old Smokey" to our sleepy babes.

Through the League and other groups that were exploring different ways to integrate society I learned about the shame we all carried for living through the days of segregation.

We all did things that rubbed against our own grains because that was the way we not only survived but moved forward.

Women, Black and White began to meet and discuss how our lives had been limited by segregation. For me having Black women meet for coffee as my guest or me as their guest to speak honestly, broke the damn of a custom that built a wall that separated us. A wall, I had known since childhood. And that wall had to come down.

I wanted to go on marches and protests and felt guilty I wasn't doing enough. But I came to realize that in my own way, I was doing my part.

One of Ted's uncles was active in the White Citizen's Council, a group of local leaders who fought integration in any way they could.

Their favorite was to call anyone who was pro-integration a communist. At the suggestion of two Jesuit priests from Ted's old high school, we formed a sodality that met weekly at Mama's old dining room table in that same large apartment off Canal Street. I was the only woman in the new group, and my role was expected to be limited to serving coffee. But I established early on that I was a vocal member, or they could all go meet somewhere else without my husband.

One of the members of the group was accused of being a communist by Ted's uncle as he, our new lawyer member, was working with his partner to start a local chapter of the ACLU in New Orleans. Ted's uncle had recently been elected to the Louisiana House and became chairman of the newly formed Un-American Activities Committee.

At Sunday dinners at my in-laws, I would challenge the six Pfister brothers on their racist beliefs, earning me the quiet respect of their wives. I had to go toe-to-toe with my aunts and Uncle L.C. who would become enraged. But I couldn't be quiet anymore, even though my newfound strength was constantly being tested.

Everything I thought was good, social security, Martin Luther King, fluoride, integration and the war in Vietnam, Mama was against. And by the time I realized how horrible that war was Mama was dead, and I couldn't tell her, "Mama, you got that damn war right."

Over time, mama would call late at night and begin yelling at me and scaring me about Cuba's Castro sending atomic bombs toward New Orleans. I told her, "I have a plan."

I did not tell her my plan was to kill my babies and myself if radiation landed anywhere nears us. She had more than a few crazy strategies, such as, drinking water from the hot water heater and hiding under the beds with sheets for protection. It reminded me of the Encanto School in Phoenix when we hid under our desks, despite the documentaries we watched of whole buildings collapsing under the weight of the winds, miles from the strike zone.

I wonder now if most Americans even knew how devastating the bombs were? Or if they, like me, were so terrorized; they considered death to be a better solution than all the survivalist novels and articles of that era?

My poor mother drove herself crazy over being excluded from communion.

Bob tried to explain to her that none of the priests at the Cathedral would refuse her communion, but she wasn't happy with that. She tried to explain to the priests that the divorce wasn't her fault, that my father was an abusive drunk.

An annulment was suggested, but that didn't please her either. It was a hurt that cut deeply into her heart and her anger at the church grew as the dictates of Vatican II circulated. She longed for fairness from the church, and there was none. The church's answer was to remove old trappings, like altar rails and altars that generations of families had paid for.

She regularly received invitations to the White House, but she refused to go because she didn't approve of President Kennedy or his wife, so instead she sent the invitations to me because she knew I would treasure them.

After his assassination, she repeatedly wrote and told me that even though she didn't like him, she didn't want him to die. Before the assassination, she was always writing or telling me in phone conversations about JFK's affairs, she even told me that Joe Kennedy paid Jackie one million dollars to stay with Jack. I would not believe any of it and by the time I read that it was all true, I just felt the waste of all our lives.

But it wasn't like Mama to apologize for her strong beliefs. She was really upset about Kennedy's death. And that wasn't like her either.

On one of her early visits to New Orleans after Cathy's birth in 1964, news came that one of the former Mayors of New Orleans, a man she intensely disliked, died in a helicopter crash.

Failing to listen to the full announcement, she exclaimed, "Thank god the bastard is dead!" Ted was standing there in shock as he exclaimed,

"Winnie his son, a young boy, died in that crash. What's wrong with you?"

"Well, of course, I didn't mean his son!" But it was another nail in all our coffins.

Remembering that scene, I couldn't understand her continued remarks about not wanting JFK to die. But then there was the strange coincidence of Julian having known Lee Harvey Oswald when we both children still lived in Covington.

Oswald's mother was a private duty nurse, and they spent summers in Covington, which gave her son more freedom during his school vacations. And I realized later that might have been why he looked so familiar. And in that time, just knowing Oswald had troubling repercussions.

At the beginning of her life in Washington, Mama was having great fun and finally meeting the people she had always known would recognize her good bones, and her family connections.

She was accepted into the Daughters of the American Revolution and then invited into the oldest DAR group of women. She wrote that the group was very exclusive, and she was one of only three Louisiana women to belong at least at that time. And Bob, a long-time member of the Washington Press Club, had a friend who wrangled a press card for her so she could attend lectures and events that excluded wives and women in general except for the few female reporters and columnists during the '60s. It was her destiny. She sent me this long description of an event that blew both of our minds.

Last week on Wed at the Press Club for male members only there was a luncheon for Otto Preminger, producer of Advise and Consent – by the way I met Allen Drury (the author) he is a member of Club also – anyway the guests were at head table, cast members Lew Ayers, Henry Fonda (what a doll), Paul Ford, George Gizzard, Eddie Hodges, my pet Chas. Laughton, Peter Crawford, Don Murray, Walter Pigeon, Gene Tierney. Since the ladies or wives of members were not asked but a few news gals of the press and TV, Bob's good friend that he lunches with most days asked me to be a special correspondent for the NY Herald Tribune. He is the new chief here; I did go and enjoyed it very much. Otto is an ass and made a double one of himself – Did you read it yet? -

    Mama became very close to the traditionalist movement begun by a Father Gommar DePauw, who made it his life's work to discredit the Vatican II movement.

    She also became obsessed with the movement for the release of the Fatima prophecies left by the Blessed Mother following her three 1917 appearances to three children in Portugal.

    Mama believed the content of the letters needed to be released so true Catholics would know that the papacy was almost dead and that when a Jesuit Cardinal from South America was elected Pope, the whole Catholic Church would fall apart. And who knows? She might have gotten that right but not because of a Jesuit though the traditionalists are doing their best to propagate that bit of blame when in truth the fall of the Catholic Church has more to do with resistance to change and accountability in the sexual abuse scandals, and protectionism of dogma that is as stale as a dead man's breath.

Dogma sets limits and God observes as we struggle with our freedom to destroy or create anew.

Before the assassination, she was becoming more and more rigid and afraid of the freedom that not only the country, but the Catholic Church was moving toward. It was the beginning of the resistance to the changes that were happening.

One of our neighbors in the Mid City section of New Orleans built a whole movement against the city's allowing for the removal of the streetcars along Canal Street from the River to the Cemeteries at the end of Canal Street. It was one of her workers who, as a splinter group, hated President Kennedy. When he heard about the shooting in Dallas, he ran to our house and banged on my front door.

"Great news, Kennedy has been shot!" I slammed the door in his face and ran through the apartment to see the news on the television. We had an old used rabbit ear television that needed silver foil to get a picture. Walter Cronkite was just announcing President Kennedy's death.

I remember kneeling on the floor in front of the television screaming and weeping and feeling like the universe had fallen apart. As it had.

I couldn't take my eyes off the pictures on the screen. Jackie leaving the hospital, her suit stained with her husband's blood.

The replay scenes of the day, the limousine, everyone looking so happy and then Jackie crawling over John, reaching her hand out to the secret service man running for the car, the car suddenly speeding away and the woman next to the man in the front seat holding him, and I couldn't make my ears catch up with what was being reported because President Kennedy was dead and it couldn't be true and yet there was the scene on the plane and the Johnson man was being sworn in as the new President.

Jackie standing there with his silly named wife, Lady Bird. And I didn't know it yet, but I would come to love that woman and her silly name, Lady Bird.

All the neighbors slowly left their televisions and gathered on porches and sidewalks to seek the safety and comfort from each other. Realizing that I was missing, Ted's Aunt Virginia came into our apartment and found me curled in a fetal position on the floor in front of our old television, where I finally found respite from the shock and grief.

"Jere, you need to pull yourself together." The sound of her voice woke me, and I remembered and began to weep again.

"Jere you are going to hurt the baby. You need to get into bed. Pregnant women can't sit or sleep on the floor."

Ted was working for a law firm by that time and came home early. Whether people liked Kennedy or not, the shock of his death, a president of the United States, made people just want to go home.

Johnson was just an old Senator, who talked funny. How could a braggart from Texas lead the country?

What would happen to the United States? What about Civil Rights? People were afraid the assassination was a Russian plot and that we might be attacked with nuclear weapons.

The Sunday after the assassination, my father-in-law and his brothers were rejoicing that someone shot the communist lover. Everyone had opinions that supported their take on the world. And then in the middle of that conversation, I went into my in-laws living room where the television was left on and witnessed Lee Harvey Oswald being shot live on a television that worked.

He had this look of surprise on his face and that reminded me of my daddy's drunken face.

Mama called me, crying, "I didn't like Kennedy, but I didn't want him dead."

I didn't believe her about not wanting Kennedy dead. At least in her imagination, she had creative ways of getting rid of people she didn't like. Those late-night phone calls were exhausting as they often woke me from much needed sleep.

"It's cheaper darling if I call after eleven. I must watch my pennies or Bob gets, (pause) funny."

In 1965, Mama's husband took her on a grand tour of Europe. She wrote me long letters about her shock with Italy. She didn't realize its beauty, its food, or its history.

I realized she was truly ignorant. That the only thing she knew about Italians was from crime movies. She returned a new woman with a whole new attitude about what was good taste and what was trash.

CHAPTER 19

No More Letters

[1966-1967]

In October of 1966, my mother called to tell me the doctor said she had breast cancer. It was a strange story of how she found out. She was at a party and asked one of her husband's friends, a surgeon, to examine one of her breasts. They went into one of the bedrooms, and he took one look and told her it was cancer and scheduled the surgery for the next week. She asked me to fly to D.C. to be with her for the mastectomy.

Ted and his mother were horrified that I would leave two toddlers. They were both sure my mother would be fine. After all, Theresa had survived. I called my doctor, who advised me to go to my mother. Aunt Laura and Harry took care of Tjohn and of course Theresa took care of her son and our daughter.

The night before Mama's surgery, she and I slept in the same room. She described her bedroom as, "My boudoir dear, every woman needs a place to herself where husbands are allowed in by invitation only."

Who talked like that? I was twenty-five and realizing my

mother was a caricature of a Southern lady and a fool. I vowed to give up my roots rather than follow in her footsteps. The young can be harsh.

Her upstairs bedroom at the front of the house had windows on three walls and a small closet next to the doorway. It was an old home built before walk-in closets. There were twin beds at one end and, at the other, a large wooden table she used as a desk. There was a dressing table and fireplace at the same end, and the desk covered with books and pamphlets and yellow pads filled with my mother's messy penmanship in her favorite shade of green ink.

I sat beside her on one of the beds as she opened her lacy, pink nightgown, and showed me the dimple on the side of her breast. That's how she described it.

"It's just a dimple, darling." The whole outside of her left breast was sunken in like the gully she had planted with succulents and tropical leaves in the house on Military Road where lived when I was small.

"This is not a dimple, Mother! This is a crevasse! Snakes are eating your breast away from the inside!" Of course, I sat silent, next to her on the side of the bed as I went back in time to my childhood and the connecting link of her most glorious garden to the water moccasins that sought shelter in its ever-abiding shade and wetness.

I was with Mama when she awoke from surgery. The first thing she told was that she was awake during the surgery and couldn't tell anyone because she was paralyzed by the drugs. Her nurse, who was standing across from me, immediately said some patients said that, but it was just a bad dream. When I told the surgeon, Mama's husband became enraged, saying, "Don't ever question one of my friends."

The doctor said it was my mother's imagination, a bad dream. He also said my mother had a metastasized cancer. I stopped breathing at that point as I realized Mama did not have her own advocate.

I knew my mother not dreaming or imagining. I could see it in her eyes. When I went back into her room, she just looked at me for a long time.

She said, "It's bad, isn't it?"

My mother, who never liked to look at the unpleasant, who was terrified all her life of ever having a mastectomy, at least in that moment, faced her death.

She fought for the sake of Clay, who was a freshman at the University of Virginia.

She had remarried for a life without worry and a little fun, and to give Clay an excellent education, and she at least succeeded in that one regard. But she was too young to die. It was terrible for her to think about abandoning her children just at the point when she might have helped us with money and status. But that was her dream. And yet, I did wonder if I might have walked away from the man and family who became such a fun and important part of my life.

That same night of the surgery, Bob told me that before the cancer was discovered, he had planned to divorce my mother. Then he moved closer to me under the guise of needing comfort. This old man, who my mother had married, was aggressive, grabbing me hard by the shoulder, as his hand reached for my breast.

It was embarrassing rather than terrifying because he had always been so proper and was in his seventies. Somehow, I got him off of me and out the bedroom door, which I locked.

I called Ted and told him what was happening. He decided it would be best for me to fly home the next night. I spent the day with Mama and made an excuse about the children. She suspected what had happened because she let me go too easily. That was the last time I saw her alive. If I had told her, would she have been surprised? Would she have blamed me as she did in the past when the boy assaulted me in the alley? Would she have been hurt? I never did tell her. But I felt such guilt in leaving.

I had a family who loved and needed me, but I knew I was leaving my mother with another man who did not love her. She was dying, and she knew she did not have her husband's love. For her, it was the second time. And worse, her belief and acceptance of a dogma that prohibited her from the communion table, the only source of comfort she had ever known.

Her incision never healed. She wrote me hopeful letters that she was going to beat this thing. I don't think she ever used the word "cancer."

She made references to her body by saying, "I'm a mess." She bought a juicer and drank large amounts of liquefied carrots. My aunts flew to Washington at separate times to be with her and finally joining forces during the last weeks and days. Years later they told me they had to beat Bob off with a broom. They laughed about it, and I was appalled and hurt they never told me. It would have been so profoundly healing for me. But I was still their niece, still "little Jere." I had not yet become my mother to these aunts of mine.

The last letter I received from Mama was short, referring to my daughter, who was in and out of the hospital in New Orleans with kidney infections and pneumonia.

"Stay with little Cappy," our private name for my daughter. "Don't worry about me–they are giving me wonderful drugs. I'm okay–love, Mom."

My aunts were already there, and I knew she was not okay. They called me the day before she died to tell me she was in liver failure, and it wouldn't be long.

When I returned to New Orleans from my short visit with Mama for her mastectomy, Cathy was diagnosed with an infection that was caused by urine refluxing back into her kidneys. Whenever this happened, she also got pneumonia. She was hospitalized three times between Thanksgiving and late January 1967. Pregnant again and exhausted, I spent every minute I could at the hospital with her. Our toddler, Tjohn, was shuttled back and forth between a neighbor and Aunt Laura and her Harry. I was such a proud mother after Cathy was born. She was never sick.

She was a good sleeper, sleeping from seven at night until five in the morning.

When she was nine months old, I noticed a persistent rash on her legs. When I pointed it out to Aunt Audrey, she suggested I contact a dermatologist. Aunt Laura and Mama demanded that I take her to an old doctor at Tulane Medical Center next to Charity Hospital. He had treated my grandmother, Winifred, who died of tuberculosis during WWII. The doctor took one look at her legs and said, "This child has asthma."

I was indignant. "How can you say that? She's never had a cold."

"She's your firstborn and not exposed to illness yet. The rash is eczema. It is a precursor to asthma. Your grandmother had it. You had asthma too when you were little."

I argued. "No one ever told me I had asthma. I had bronchitis and earaches."

I left the doctor's office with my baby girl, thinking the doctor was crazy, old, and senile. He prescribed an ointment for the rash, and I set out to prove him wrong. But I never did prove the old man wrong.

Our lovely daughter soon developed Asthma as did I.

Going back in time a bit, to our son, Tjohn's birth fourteen months after Cathy's birth. He could not sleep at night. Mama and Bob were on their European tour of Europe. Six weeks after his birth I was readmitted to the hospital with pneumonia and exhaustion and a few days later, rushed back home because Hurricane Betsy was heading straight for us and knocking down oak trees limbs and power lines and flooding low-lying areas of East New Orleans. The windows of our apartment were not properly sealed, and wind-driven rain filled our living room as Ted and I pushed towels and newspapers around the frames. Our babies slept through the storm thanks to liquid Benadryl. Ted and I did not. Hurricanes are terrifying because you have no control due to the winds and the sounds.

LIKE A FISH DENIED A RIVER

We lived on a tree-lined street, and the sound of breaking limbs and branches flying against the house kept us awake and fearful. There was no news, as the radio and television stations were all down. And of course, we lost electricity and didn't get it back for three weeks.

During the short visit to the hospital before the storm, they discovered I was pregnant again. At first, I was horrified at the thought of having a third baby so quickly, and then, just as I talked myself into it; I began to hemorrhage.

A neighbor took the two babies, and my teenage babysitter drove my car to the hospital. She had just learned to drive and was scared to death, but when Ted arrived at the hospital, the doctor told him, "Go home; I will be fine."

Left alone in my private hospital room, I felt something exceptionally large come out of me and thankfully had the presence of mind to push the call button. The large something was a huge blood clot, and I was rushed to surgery.

When I woke up, I asked where they kept the remains of my baby, the nurse looked at me like I was crazy and said, "Honey there was just a lot of blood and broken up placenta and fetal tissue and we just flushed it into the sewer system."

I include that dialogue because it was a Catholic hospital run by women who had common sense, unlike some state legislatures that demand that all fetal material be buried in a cemetery. But at that point all I felt was guilt that it was my fault my baby died. I really did not want that baby, no matter how I tried to lie to myself. It was too soon.

The good part of the ordeal was that I quickly found a new doctor and hospital that were fully air-conditioned.

Ted's mother and grandmother were a godsend during those days of two babies at once. As soon as I entered their home, Grandma took baby Tjohn and Theresa took Cathy. We put those babies down for a nap and I would join mother and daughter at the kitchen table where I listened as mother-in-law, now called Nana, would talk about the sadness and hurt of her childhood at her father's hands as she tried to make sense of her life.

Grandma would listen and never try to defend herself or her long-deceased husband. I didn't realize it yet, but Theresa was the scapegoat child in her father's home, and like so many mothers, the beloved grandma was unable to help protect her oldest daughter.

We never just sat at the table talking. Our hands were busy shelling peas or snapping green beans or peeling shrimp. Food that was in season was purchased by the bushel. New Orleans had neighborhood stores, and the owner would call and tell you what was available. The butcher would order ham bones if that was a suitable seasoning for a vegetable or for whatever the main meal might be. So not only was I getting help with my babies, but I was also getting free food to take home, and more importantly I was learning about being a woman. Real women talked about personal things without covering up hurts with laughter. There were no secrets.

By late January 1967, I knew I was losing my mother, and I soon lost my usual help from Ted's mother, who now had her hands full taking care of Grandma, who had developed dementia and couldn't be left alone.

Even when the weather was warm, Grandma would turn the gas heater on in her bedroom, making her bedroom stifling hot, but then she started turning the gas on and forgetting to light it. Grandma was moved to a nursing home only to have another daughter decide she could take care of her mother better than her sister or a nursing home could and turned her shotgun apartment's dining room into a bedroom for Grandma. That lasted less than a week, when she was forced to acknowledge defeat. Grandma was moved back into a nursing home, causing her to lose even more ground.

CHAPTER 20

Mama (Part 2)

I turned twenty-six on February 19, 1967. A week later, Mama was dead. I was pregnant again and Cathy was well enough for me to leave her, so Ted bought me a flight to Dulles the next day.

I left Cathy and Tjohn with Ted and his mother, who was free now. Julian says he picked me up at the airport. Somehow, I blocked him out of that time.

Years later, Clay had to tell me Julian was at Mother's funeral before I would believe it. As usual, Julian was pushing away what he didn't want to see and using sarcasm as a block. I didn't remember him driving us to the funeral home in downtown Washington because I was still mentally with Ted and my two toddlers, unlike most travels away from home, when I greeted whatever new adventure was about to begin. I kept thinking, "How can Mama be dead at forty-nine?"

I do remember my three aunts, Billie, Ellen, and Laura, sitting in straight, back chairs against the opposite wall from the open coffin. I wouldn't go near the coffin.

Even from the doorway, I could see Mama's body was swollen

and bloated. She was dressed in a maroon housecoat with a bouquet of fresh violets in her folded hands. She looked like a whore in an old Western movie, lying in her coffin in a strange, formal, dark funeral home parlor in downtown D.C. Its walls covered in ancient, red-flocked wallpaper.

I stood in the doorway staring at my aunts. "This is not what Mother wanted. She wanted to be buried in a closed casket."

Aunt Laura said, "Lower your voice."

Ellen said, "It is what Bob wanted. He's her husband."

Billie said, "Just come and sit with us, Jere, it will make you feel better."

Ellen took my hand in hers "All we have to do is get through this."

So, I did. I put one foot in front of the other. My mother's funeral was in the same Catholic Cathedral as was President Kennedy.

In a bit of irony, her coffin sat in the middle of a rectangle memorializing the President she most hated. Father DePauw was there but was not allowed to say the funeral Mass or to stand at the main altar as she requested, so he stood by himself saying the old Latin Mass at a side altar.

When it was time to go up to Communion, my aunts tried to stop me by stepping around them, so I crawled over their bodies. Of course, Bob was bothered by the disturbance to his beloved wife's funeral service.

Following the funeral, a long line of limousines followed the one bearing the coffin. I hated the idea of mother being buried among strangers. I remember it was very cold, and the borrowed maternity dress I was wearing under my coat was too thin for the weather.

There was an expanse of green across from Mama's grave, and I thought we were in the country. I remember the grave was owned by her husband's family. He planned to be buried next to his son and first wife in Arlington Cemetery.

When Mama died, I did not walk away from the house with any of her pretty silver pieces or her white China with rich blue and silver rings.

I did not take the beautiful umbrella with the brass handle she found in a junk shop on Magazine Street. The two of us spent a whole night polishing that handle and then she brought it to the umbrella repair shop in the French Quarter to have new black material and spokes made. As I was leaving with it, Bob stopped me, saying it reminded him of his dear wife. I should have hit him with it, but I didn't have the energy. I was still an overly polite young woman, a child really, with small children who needed me to become the woman I longed to be and would become.

Shortly after her death, a package arrived addressed to me. It contained the red leather purse she bought soon after her marriage to Bob. Inside it were yellow "Top Value" saving stamps, which in the fifties and sixties were like grocery coupons you pasted inside the coupon book, so you could trade them for merchandise. There were just enough books for the bassinet I had always wanted for my newborns. I was pregnant and three years later would be again. Two of my babies got to sleep in the final gift from Mama.

That bassinet turned out to be an inheritance that kept giving, as six of my eight grandchildren and more of my cousin's children and grandchildren, to a total of thirty babies have spent time in that little bed. And I still have the red leather purse with a single yellow "Top Value" stamp tucked into the mirror holder.

Ted disliked my mother for good reason. But the rule against speaking ill of the dead was a strongly held belief for him. And because he couldn't reconcile his belief with his relief that my mother was dead, it caused him to have a nervous breakdown.

Which in turn shut down any discussion of my mixed feelings and my ability to grieve. So, when Aunt Laura's husband died on Mother's Day 1967 I broke down crying when Uncle L.C. called.

I had not yet cried for Mama. It was still too soon. So, I took all my grief and, like an angry baseball player; I threw it hard against the dead man we called Harry. The sisters all said I was overreacting, being dramatic. How I hated that phrase. Such a denial of my pain, and my grief, and my tears.

They never considered that I might grieve for this man who had loved my son Tjohn like his grandparents hadn't. It was Harry who bought him beautiful corduroy overalls, striped shirts, and heavy socks with bands of color around the cuffs. They never considered that the day he died was the day we celebrate our mothers and that I might be grieving for my mother, even if I didn't yet know the reason for my terrible grief.

They never considered that Harry, whose own mother died the previous Christmas, might have missed his mother that much. Harry died of a heart attack.

A month later, I remember sitting on the sofa next to my husband on the warm June night before our new baby was born. I couldn't tell the man I married how relieved I was that my mother was dead. I couldn't tell anyone.

The heaviness of avoiding any conversation about my feelings filled me, weighed me down. I decided to kill myself, right then and there.

I remember pulling myself up to a standing position and thinking, "Now, how am I going to do this?"

At that moment, my water broke. Just like that. There was this flowing water running down my legs, and I just stood in it. It felt soft, like warm baby oil soothing me, and releasing the weight of my sorrow. There was no question it was the summer solstice, and I was going to live and give birth. It was enough.

CHAPTER 21
The Alone Years

[1967 - 1973]

Ted panicked and called a neighbor's daughter to watch the children while he took me to our new hospital.

Labor hadn't really begun, so Ted was encouraged to go home so he could bring the children to his mother in the morning. I spent my labor alone for the most part. Nurses and residents checked in on me. The on-call doctor was concerned because the baby wasn't positioned correctly. He tried turning the baby, but it was stuck.

It still didn't have a name or a gender. They wanted to give me an epidural. I remember at least three young men with concerned faces standing over me telling me how my labor might be long and painful. They finally left me alone for a bit and I slept until morning.

My new doctor was standing over me and Ted was sitting by my bed, waiting for me to wake up. I had slept through most of my labor. But it was time. The delivery room was filled with early sunlight and there was the mirror I had wanted for previous births. As I was put into the stirrups, the contractions were strong. All these men, except for Ted were surrounding me. Husbands weren't allowed in the delivery room yet.

"Look, Jere, the baby is crowning."

"Open your eyes."

I couldn't believe what I was seeing was connected to me, my body. My vulva was huge.

"Come on, open those eyes." I did. I was panting fast as the contractions were growing stronger. The first thing I saw was a tiny testicle. My new baby was born with heels over his head.

Someone shouted, "It's a boy?!" I felt like I was having a huge bowel movement.

My doctor said, "Jere, I'm going to have to cut you." But it shouldn't hurt." He was being technical, and I was still grunting, but my whole being was filled with laughter. And my new baby boy was born. He was so blue he looked black. But hanging upside down, held by the strong hands of the delivering doctor, he started screaming. And then everyone was laughing.

"I'm going to put him on your chest right away. He's too little and it will be awhile before you can hold him. But he's going to live. He's a fighter."

The nurses on the delivery floor said I would never nurse him and tried to give me a pill to stop the milk from flowing. The nurses on the post-partum said the same over and over. But my neighbor brought me a handheld breast pump and when they took away my empty coffee cup, I poured the milk into my dirty ashtray. It's true new mothers could smoke in their hospital rooms. I pleaded with the doctors and nurses

"Couldn't I just freeze my breast milk until he came home?"

"NO!" In unison this was their response.

I left the hospital on the second day so I wouldn't lose my sanity. The answer was always no, to any of my inquiries.

The La Leche League wasn't there yet when I needed them. But I pumped my breasts for six weeks until Robby got home. And every night after supper we visited, but we had to stand outside in the hallway and look through a window at our baby inside of the incubator.

Once home, I had the guilty pleasure of rest. We had bought a house in a subdivision in a new community across the Mississippi River that was still under construction.

We moved in, in early September. Robby was barely three months old then. He had to be fed every three hours. And it took forty-five minutes for him to suck four ounces of milk. He wasn't strong enough to suckle from my breast, so I pumped my breast, beginning with two ounces in the first weeks. He even needed a tiny nipple that was red and soft enough for him to pull milk into his body.

The neighborhood was filled with young families, and the wives of officers in Vietnam, who supplemented their income by teaching at the local grade school. Cathy and Tjohn tried to help me and one morning while I fell asleep with the baby, they waxed the new brown vinyl kitchen floor with Elmers Glue. They were so proud of themselves as they showed me the god-awful mess. All I could do was hug them. Two neighbors came over and helped me clean up the floor while the children napped. Gradually things got better, Robby grew stronger and was a happy little baby.

Cathy was still sucking on a pacifier, and so was her younger brother. And they both liked to take a bottle to bed with them.

One Sunday, she announced she was giving up on both her bottle and pacifier the next day. Sure enough, on Monday, she got up and carried her bottle and pacifier past me into the garage and threw them both in the garbage can. The next morning, without saying a word, her little brother came out of his room carrying his habits and threw them in the same can. Same with potty training, Cathy was first, Tjohn followed a week later.

Gradually Robby grew stronger and graduated to a bottle with a regular nipple and began eating baby food right on time.

. . .

He was a happy baby and at nine months began pulling himself up onto the rails of his crib. And then he and Tjohn both got pneumonia and had to be hospitalized. There was an epidemic of children with pneumonia, and the hospital was filled with sick and dying children right at Mardi Gras time.

For two nights, both boys were separated, meaning both Ted and I had to take turns staying with each of our sons. Luckily, they survived, but after Robby's release, his whole development changed. He couldn't pull up anymore and he was a slow crawler. But the most disturbing thing was his disposition. He became an angry baby who could no longer sleep through the night.

By the time he was three, he could walk, but the anger and screaming continued. I knew about autism, but an older neighbor told me to never use that word. The mother was always to blame. When he was three, I introduced him to his baby brother, who was born at high noon on the 4th of July.

Robby began pounding on me with his little fists. Somehow, I knew he felt abandoned and was fearful I'd never come back. I never doubted that he wanted to please me. Another neighbor was running a preschool with a little desk for each child. She took him on but cautioned me to have him checked.

The pediatrician said, "Look Jere, two out of three ain't bad."

Robby didn't cause trouble at the preschool. The teacher just had a good eye. But her communication skills were lacking as she did not report on what she was seeing that might be abnormal. But gradually I couldn't hide from his problems, I just didn't know what to do.

After lunch, he spent hours outside running in circles, holding on to the trunk of one of the trees in the back yard, and screaming at the top of his lungs. If he was inside, he was rocking back and forth, screaming.

Afraid he would hurt himself; I got him a rocker. And over time, I came to realize he didn't feel pain when he hurt himself. And he couldn't talk. He had ear infections. So, at four I allowed the ear doctor to do a tonsillectomy.

After the surgery, he began talking. But the surgeon was worried . Once again, no one gave me specific or helpful information. I did know that if I, in utter frustration, cried, Robby would stand next to me, patting my leg or hand, staring at me. It was the only time I could give him a hug.

And then I was pregnant again. For much of my pregnancy with Phil, Ted was living in Baton Rouge as his company loaned him to the State. And later he became the Louisiana Lobbyist representing his company.

Aunt Billie visited quite a bit sometimes with Uncle Scottie. She and I were becoming closer friends. And the children all loved her and Scottie.

I really needed their help as Nana and Paw would begin to come less and less, as she was having trouble with food. She kept copious notes on what foods she ate and how certain foods affected her digestive system. She began to lose weight and was in a lot of pain.

Shortly after Phillip's birth in 1970, Theresa called and asked me to help with making her bed. She had been in the hospital for tests.

I found someone not too far away. It was early August, and school would be starting soon, so mothers were shopping for school clothes and extra dollars were welcome. I had to take Phil with me, as he was still tiny. I was still exhausted from giving birth, because Robby couldn't sleep anymore, and Phil needed a feeding during the night. But Theresa had never asked me for help before and packing the baby into a new car bed, off we went.

While Theresa sat in a chair holding a tiny Phil, I put clean sheets on her bed. Then we got to the real reason for my being there without the other children.

Theresa wanted to bless me. And God, I needed a blessing. She told me how much she admired me for taking care of not only my children, without a mother and her son.

She knew he was a difficult man and she had watched me balance his work without complaining. And now she was leaving me with another difficult man, her husband. She hoped I would invite him to dinner on Sundays. I promised I would, though I couldn't promise to cook spaghetti and fried chicken and twice-baked potatoes.

"He's going to ask you too." She said.

"Don't ever promise or cook like me because once you start, you can't stop. Tell him and stick to your pleasure."

And then she gave me the supreme compliment.

"You have turned into an excellent cook."

She had been ill for the past year. Misdiagnosed, she had colon cancer and soon died a very painful death.

Cathy was six when her beloved Nana died, and I will go to my grave sorrowful that I didn't allow her to attend Theresa's wake or funeral.

When my father's mother, Nonnie died, I was not allowed to attend her funeral but if I had, I might have understood death and the rituals surrounding death as a way of comforting the bereaved.

I loved my Nonnie because she was the one who prepared me for school, when I yelled out, "Come wipe me!" She taught me how to wipe myself after a bowel movement at a time when mama didn't allow me to clean myself in case I wound up touching myself in that forbidden place.

The Easter before my grandfather died, she picked out half a dozen dyed Easter chicks that were in a large cage near the exit to my grandfather's hardware store.

My mother had refused to allow us to have them because she knew the dye was poisonous and would kill the chicks.

Nonnie knew they would die also, but probably thought it was a good way to teach me about one of the facts of life. Everything dies. And God Bless her, she tried.

When the chicks began to die, they just disappeared. But when I found my favorite chick, the one that was a bright yellow, I was inconsolable.

She took me to the back porch where she kept her trowels. And then, holding my hand tightly, we crossed the street in front of her house and went through the wooden turnstile to a spot where cherry tomatoes grew and there was a water spigot to wash them with.

She dug a small hole with her trowel and placed the dead chick, now wrapped in a piece of cloth, in the hole and covered it with dirt. She explained that every creature that died and wasn't for the table had to be buried.

I allowed her the ritual, but the next day I took my breakfast spoon and crossed the street by myself and dug up my chick. When I unwrapped it, its head hung at a strange angle and the fluffy feathers were matted and came off in my hand when I tried to make her like before. Nonnie had watched me leave and made sure I crossed the street safely. I was crying and trying to make my chick live again.

She took one of her beautiful handkerchiefs that she kept pinned to her lapel. She placed the remains of my chick into the cloth once more. And helped me rebury it. Then she washed my hands and face from the spigot and fed me the washed cherry tomatoes to soothe my grief.

I always imagined that the place where my little chick was buried was an empty lot. Years later, I learned that both my grandparents and their daughter played tennis. There was a clay court and a wooden stand for viewers and waiting tennis players who sat watching the matches.

My grandfather was the president of the Draft Board. With the onset of WWII, the town and country were in grief and had little interest in playing tennis when so many young men were dying on foreign soil. I do not think it was ever used again.

. . .

New Orleans didn't provide kindergarten, but churches did. The Baptists in Algiers across the river from New Orleans Central ran an excellent school. Two days after the start of classes, I was called in for a conference regarding behavior they observed concerning Robby.

They noticed he was unable to move forward or around obstacles in his path. He would just freeze. They gave me the name and a high recommendation to a neuro-pediatric psychiatrist, Dr. Walter Robinson. With our first appointment, I was impressed and insisted Ted go with me and our son to the next appointment. I knew we had to both be on board with whatever treatment the doctor recommended.

Dr. Robinson never used the word *autism*, but he sent us to a children's psychologist for testing who gave me good advice but diagnosed me as an *icebox mother*?

A pejorative term, I understand, is back in use. I was so loving toward Robby and all of my children. But as I would discover over time, I did hide my emotions.

I just didn't know what to do. And I felt such guilt over my mothering skills but Dr. Robinson reassured me that none of Robby's symptoms and acting out were my fault. It was genetic. That was a new term for me.

The main medication he prescribed was Dexedrine. Ritalin had just reached the market, but this doctor preferred a pill that could be broken into quarters if necessary.

There were other medications whose names I can't remember, but the crux was Robby became calmer and felt better. He still needed his rocker and time to vent his frustrations, but he was able to function at school. I was getting good reports from his teachers. I was worried over his future education and called a friend who had recently earned a doctorate in Special Education.

Should I send Robby to a Catholic or a public school? Her advice was quick and clear.

"Move to another state."

CHAPTER 22
Michigan

[1973 - 1978]

Two days later, Ted got a big raise and a transfer to Lansing, Michigan.

If you have to move across the country, a corporate move is the way to go. The company paid for our new house buying trip and then moved our car and furniture, and the whole caboodle into our new home.

It even packed and unpacked our belongings. Our new home was a cape cod with a two-car-attached garage, two fireplaces and a three-quarter-acre lot that had a sled hill and a flat area in the back yard that was a perfect baseball diamond. And best of all, the neighbors welcomed us and made life so much easier than we had ever experienced in the south.

Our neighbor next-door was a urologist. And as Cathy had to have frequent urine tests this came in as an unexpected convenience.

"Just bring a specimen in a jar or a glass in the morning and I'll take care of it."

The Johnson's were a no-nonsense couple. It took a while before I collected any jars, so in freezing wintry weather I would walk to their front door holding a mug of steaming urine. I would knock on the door and a hand would reach out and yell thank you as they grabbed the jar and disappeared back inside the house.

Mr. Smith, on the other side of our property, was a weed specialist from Michigan State and recommended that we allow the weeds to grow.

"No need to dig them up. They add color all summer. Grass is a waste."

Because it was April, I went to the nearby school to register the children and talk to someone about holding Robby back a year in kindergarten.

Cathy and Tjohn wanted to go to school and meet their new classmates. The principal replied it wasn't their policy, but she could arrange for testing at the district offices which were a bike ride away.

Robby couldn't ride a bike yet without training wheels, so while his brother and sister were in class, he made it his business to learn to ride one of their bicycles.

And he did and the next day he was the owner of a two-wheel bike, so when the time for the test came later in the summer, he rode himself.

Robby did repeat a grade and was admitted to a remedial motor clinic at Michigan State. For the cost of $18 a semester he got one-on-one attention from a graduate student. And he also had the benefit of Special Education assistance for the next twelve years.

In second grade, he learned to read and write. His first assignment was to write a letter to someone. The salutation began, Hi Mom.

There were lines going from left to right, then right to left. Those words were backwards. That is when I knew he was going to be okay. He stood in front of me as I read the letter, then I looked up and, smiling told him, "Oh Robby, you can write." I hugged him and for the first time, he hugged me back. And that was all both of us needed.

The front yard had two large maple trees that dropped a ton of leaves in the fall which the kids raked into big stacks that could soften their falls. They, along with neighboring children, jumped into the leaves scattering them over-and-over again.

Then a neighbor who was from Germany brought bags for the kids to fill and haul to her backyard where she raised rabbits for the table.

We had a walkout basement, and the one sofa and coffee table went downstairs along with our lone television set.

I joined the League of Women Voters, and the members all brought folding chairs as we had the monthly unit meeting in our living room, where they left the chairs neatly folded against the wall until the next meeting.

Another neighbor showed me how to drive on ice and snow, and another got me to drive and deliver meals on wheels to the elderly and handicapped.

By the end of that first fall, I was an accepted and fully vested member of the community.

Another newcomer moved into the house next to the weed man. Dorothy had four little boys the same ages as my kids, and her house had a pool but no one in the family knew how to swim, so I taught them.

And then when winter arrived, there was a pond one street over that froze every year where we all learned to ice skate.

And most important, I could finally breathe without anyone telling me what was proper or cautioning me not to think or make comments about what was proper or Catholic.

Aunt Billie and Uncle Scottie came twice, but their visits were short and as much as I loved them, I preferred Billie's long letters with perfect penmanship about life on the farm with Uncle Scottie who loved nature and his cows. The letters also contained news of Laura and Hank, and Covington.

If Uncle Scottie had lived out west or in Texas, he would be known as a cattle rancher. But he was a farmer too.

He borrowed a lot of money and bought the machines for

harvesting hay and making the rows of earth for and seeding the land. He had a machine that cut and tied the hay, and another attachment for planting and harvesting corn. His problem with the cattle was he didn't like killing his animals. He loved raising special breeds of chickens and roosters but not for the table.

Ted and I and our children loved going to the farm. It always looked like hillbilly land.

Their house was made of cedar and never painted. Neighbors could borrow tools out of their barn but taking anything off the front porch was stealing. Ergo, front porches in Mississippi were crowded with anything valuable.

Billie filled her letters with all the happenings on the farm. Scottie getting up at all hours shooting his shotgun to scare away predators, both beast and human. There were stories of helping birth calves stuck in the vaginal canals of their mothers.

Away from fighting with Mama and the Federal Government bureaucracy, her sense of humor came alive in those long letters. During our Michigan years, she was happy.

Our first winter in Michigan, I received a call from her during a unit meeting of the League. She and Scottie were on a train that would arrive the next morning in Chicago. It was during the January thaw. I'll give her that. She hadn't told me her plans, and it was in the days before cell phones.

"Billie, that's at least a four-or-five-hour drive."

"I thought it was closer. I got to go, pick us up."

That was it. My aunt had total trust I would be there. I was in shock. Ted was out of town as usual when anything went wrong. But the League women came through. I was given a map. A hotel reservation across from the train station that I could afford. They even gave me some cash. Ted's secretary agreed to take off work early, be there when kids arrived home from school, and tell Ted what happened. And I was off.

. . .

By the time I reached the hotel, it was dark. I had filled the gas tank before I left, so gas wasn't a problem. I checked into my hotel room, which reminded me of the old Southern Hotel in Covington where Daddy stayed when he couldn't come home.

The room was long and narrow with a small bath and shower. It also had a narrow closet to hang a suit and coat. There was a single bed.

I called home and everything was good there. Phil wasn't in school yet but was still having fun with an older Johnson boy next door.

I was hungry, and it was my drink time. The recommended eatery was down the street, so I walked. I had never been alone in my life. I was the mother of four children. I suddenly realized this marked me as a grown-up woman.

My whole body was tingling with excitement. I changed into a nicer sweater and left my room, carefully locking the door. As ever, I talked too much to the waiter and told him it was my first adventure on my own. I had two martinis, and the manager walked me halfway back to the hotel.

Inside my room, I locked the door and placed a chair under the doorknob. Then I got into bed and realized I hadn't brought anything to read. The television didn't work and there wasn't even a bible in the bedside table. I read myself to sleep with the Chicago telephone book. The train was four hours late, so I drove the car to the Lake Front and explored the city through the snakelike streets. Billie and Scottie arrived around noon.

I amazed them with my driving through a strange city and as soon as we crossed into Michigan the first major snowstorm of 1974 hit. Thankfully, there were the big fluffy flakes of snow, but my windshield wipers were not working and I had to open my window and use my snow brush to wipe the snow off the windshield until we found a gas station that had the size we needed.

Scottie eventually replaced my worn-out wipers, and for the rest of my life, I had to listen as Billie proudly told the saga of Jere driving down the highway, wiping her window clean of snow.

"Like it was the most natural thing in the world."
And I would reply, "Well, I learned from the best."

It was in the first months that I could finally grieve my mother's life and death.

I began by taking her with us on our adventures as we traveled with the children throughout Michigan. Our first long trip was to the Upper Peninsula. It was late September and by the time we reached the narrow bridge of land, shadows began to fall from the trees.

At the first road stop, the children were more than ready for an active stop. Before Ted or I could stop them, they were out of the car and running down a wooded path to the shoreline between Lake Michigan and Lake Superior.

I ran ahead of Ted to reach the children before they ran into the Lake. When I got to them, they were just standing in a line, silent. And like them I was struck dumb, in awe I saw this huge sun as it sank into the horizon of Lake Superior. When Ted reached us, he too went silent. I have no idea how long we stood there, two adults and four-step ladder children. I do remember Robby breaking the silence.

"Are we in California yet?"

"Not yet Robby. We're someplace better for now, anyway. We're still in Michigan."

Robby was enthralled with cowboy ads on television. I just kept telling him we were on the road to California. And eventually he would move there with his wife.

We stayed in a motel that night. It had a wood-burning stove and a television. We had sleeping bags for the kids. There were no McDonalds in the U.P. back then. But there were bars everywhere that welcomed families. They served hamburgers and Pasties; little pies filled with stew meat and gravy. Back in the mining days, the women would put them in their husband's buckets to heat up on their shovel held out over their lanterns.

Looking back, I don't think I was ever lonely in Michigan. Ted frequently traveled, and that could be frustrating at times. But I finally found a home inside of myself.

After his father's stroke Ted turned over the checkbook and old savings account book.

He was not a good manager due to his fear of making a mistake. I already knew that fear from childhood but remembered Aunt Billie's and Mama's fights over money. I opened my own savings account and before I paid bill number one, I deposited at least ten dollars into my account and if there was any left over, at least half of that amount went into my savings.

We no longer fought over money, and I could budget and plan better for when to buy school clothes and shoes.

When the snow melted, the mud was unbelievable. The hardware store sold used ice skates and if you traded them in, you received a larger discount.

The same with mud shoes. The shopping area within three long blocks was a village.

There was a library, a gas station, an ice cream shop, a drugstore, an upscale beauty parlor, a small grocery and a meat market. A Meyer Thrifty Acres was behind the village where I bought blankets and snow boots that served as mud boots during thaws. There was also a shopping mall with a movie theater across the road. Even the drive to downtown Lansing was short. Ted's office was across from the Capitol.

When his father was recovered enough to travel, he would come for three or four months every year. He would come down after the children went to school or left to spend the day playing with their friends, outside.

By that time, all my morning chores were done. I'd sit with him while he drank his coffee and ate a small breakfast. There was a divider between the dining and living rooms where I kept several porcelain plates that were Mama's.

One morning while we were visiting, I broke down and began to cry.

"I didn't know you ever cried," he said.

Shocked, I replied, "I cry all the time."

"In all the years I have known you, I have never seen you cry. Not even when your mother died."

"I couldn't cry then. I didn't have time. I was numb. I cried more after Nana died."

"I didn't know, Jere."

As I picked up the shattered pieces of porcelain, I knew something had changed between us. And more importantly inside of me. I thought tears would make me appear weak. Instead, the lack of tears made me seem cold, like I had no emotions. Just being dramatic.

It would take time, but by the time he died seventeen years later, we were deeply connected. And by that time, the shell I had built to protect me from grief was forever gone. But that would come later. ButI had my first clue to beginning to understand how others might see me. Even my children.

Once a month Ted traveled to the Natural Resource Commission monthly meetings. Sometimes, I went with him and kept notes for the League of Women Voters.

Over the five years, he had two secretaries. Always needing extra money, both were more than willing to stay with the children. While Ted was busy lobbying for oil and gas, which I had to be a part of at dinners, but during the side meetings, I gravitated to the Sierra Club representatives.

I had never heard the term Land Use until we moved to

Michigan. But Michigan had a unique history. The whole State of Michigan was once filled with primeval forests.

When Chicago burned, the whole of Michigan was clear cut to rebuild the city of Chicago. One stand of original trees remained in Michigan, the Pigeon River Forest. And that was where the largest reserve of oil lay waiting for the drillers.

Ted was sent to be the lobbyist for his company, but there was too much work required. He had to hire local law firms and work with the other drilling companies that formed an association and so we entertained a great deal. There was a lot of drinking which I was partial to. It was the time of three martini lunches for businessmen.

CHAPTER 23
A Horrid Death

[1978]

I must go back in time a bit to explore all the factors of Mama's death. All through my early twenties, I tried to stay in relationship with my father.

My first-born son took his first steps in the house our father shared with his wife Boots. It was a tiny house, and I'm not sure how we all managed.

Ted and I slept in twin beds in the master bedroom. Our oldest son was a climber, pulling out drawers and bookcases over on to him. He was never seriously hurt, but during this visit, he pulled a bottom drawer out of my father's chest and found a loaded pistol. I have no idea of the caliber, but on his unsteady legs, our Tjohn carried the gun into the kitchen where the adults were all talking. Boots shouted at my father, "Smithy, I told you to put that thing on a top shelf in the closet!"

I never took a child back to that house. I remember thinking it was going to be different someday and he, my father, would become a good father and would want to know and be a part of my life. I cannot believe I really fell for my dream or even desired it. The fact remains; it never happened.

Shortly after our mother's funeral, I received a call from our father asking me if he could finally rejoin his membership in the Knights of Columbus and mentioned his former status as a Grand Knight.

"Why ask me that?"

"I know you are active in the church and could check it out for me."

"That's for you to do, Daddy. You haven't called to offer any condolences. And I just found out you tried to stop sending Clay the money he is due."

"That Bastard she married threatened to take me to court! I can't be expected to go on supporting two families."

"Daddy, you left our mother when she had tuberculosis, and we were all young." He hung up.

A few months later, I received a letter my father wrote to the son of the lawyer who took care of our parents' divorce.

It was meant to disown Clay, who had almost no memory of him, for choosing to attend the University of Virginia over accepting his offer to live with our father's new family and attend McNeese College in Lake Charles. The letter also included a tirade against Clay for not sending him, his loving father, a thank you note for the gift of a set of old golf clubs.

I called my father immediately and told him I had received a copy of the letter from the lawyer and if he ever followed through on his treat to disown Clay, I would never speak to him again.

It never dawned on him that neither of his sons might want to play the game of gentlemen with clubs and tiny balls. And it certainly never dawned on him that I might take up the game. But the biggest hurt was how our father used the inuendo that Clay wasn't his son as a means of calming his conscious in leaving all of us when our mother was too ill to care for us.

When, in 1973, my family moved to Michigan. I thought I would be free of my father. But the phone would ring, and it would be

Daddy's drunken voice, telling me about terrible accidents or how he was going to take his gun and shoot the bastard husband of one of his stepdaughters.

He told me all his new family's business but never asked about mine. Nor did he want to hear if I tried to interject. The migraine headache would start midway through his monologue. I wonder now if his father treated him in a similar manner. At least that was Mama's excuse for our father's irresponsibility.

Twice I flew from Michigan to Lake Charles. The first time, the summer of 1976, because he had open heart surgery after discovering his left thumb had developed gangrene; the second time was in 1978 when I went in response to a stroke he suffered while going through an angiogram.

It was early spring or late winter, with terrible ice storms that year. Ted drove me to the Detroit Airport. I didn't want to go, but the command about honoring my father kept running through my head. I had terrible arguments with myself. How could I be compelled to honor him? But then I realized I was really going for Cindy and Boots. That made it better. I had grown to respect Boots, who never made excuses and Cindy who was a sweet little sister. By the time I arrived, he was in a coma. His left arm was black from gangrene. The doctor wanted to amputate.

I whispered in his ear, "I'm here Daddy, I'm sorry this has happened to you, and I came to tell you goodbye. I love you."

Love was not a truthful word for what I felt for him, which in the end was rage disguised as compassion. The kind of love you have for someone who you would like to write off or hate or worse, ignore, but something stops you. Was it humanity? I don't know the answer. I was still young.

In the waiting room, his friends were begging the doctor to leave his arm on, not to amputate because he would need it.

"He plays golf every day, man!"

. . .

I'm fascinated by his friends. They could not bring themselves to accept their golf and drinking buddy's approaching death.

They brought him cold beer and left it on the floor next to his bed in the ICU as an offering before falling to their knees in prayer.

The doctor did amputate my father's arm. But by the time my father returned from surgery, his feet had turned black.

I remember pulling back the sheet and asking the doctor if he might place my father in a private room so his many friends and family could stay with him. That was the only way I could think to leave. I never did see him in his own room.

Later, I heard the chaplain sat with his friends and family, encouraging them to tell stories and laugh and speak directly to this dying man they loved in life.

The man who romanced me as a child and couldn't quite break the memory of a sweet little compliant girl child to his affections.

The irony was too much. My mother died alone when her sisters left her alone to have drinks and dinner, and my father was surrounded by stories and love that I was not a part of.

What stories did my aunts tell as my mother lay dying? I don't remember any of them laughing except at the cocktail hour. Did they tell each other stories of their childhood? When they told stories with me present, the stories were about other people, never themselves.

Shortly after speaking to the doctor, I flew back to Michigan and into another ice storm.

A few days later Cindy called to say our father had died and would I come back for the funeral? I reminded her that I had already said goodbye and two ice storms were enough. I fooled myself into thinking I could make the dead die. I legally renounced all rights to any inheritance from my father and still he did not die. The longing for a loving father held me like a wrench threatening to break my love for any man.

Several years later, I fell down a flight of stairs and broke my leg. I was surrounded by men, doctors and physical therapists and patients like the retired football players who had young grandsons trying to help their forty-something gramps move again.

I realized that all the chains of entrapment had to be broken.

It took a two-week trip to New Mexico in the company of women and immersion into the Rio Grande and being stung by a yellow jacket for my eyes and brain to open to the possibility that there were older and stronger truths to follow than the ones that had informed my life up until that point.

Throughout my fifties, I continued to journey back to that land of the ancient ocean bed. I am a Pisces.

CHAPTER 24

The Making of A Ghost

[1977 - 1995]

After Aunt Laura's husband died, she sold their house in New Orleans. Harry had little insurance, and he spent every dime he made on their living expenses.

He was a freelance insurance adjuster for large shipping companies. That would explain how they met. Laura worked for insurance companies for many years, so she understood the business and sold it to one of his competitors for an acceptable price.

After selling their home she moved to Bay St. Louis, Mississippi, where she and her sisters had spent many summers as children and promptly found a job writing insurance for a small one-man office.

She set out to make a good life for their only son, Hank.

She bought a lovely little house with a huge oak tree whose sheltering branches hung over the house. It was in an old neighborhood on the protected ridge where the town of Bay St. Louis was originally settled.

Hank was only ten and grieved his father. Harry had read him to sleep every night until his death. He did okay in school and made friends easily. He was a kid who loved to play and if you were lucky enough to live on the Bay the world of water sports prevailed. There were no malls, so when he was sixteen, Laura bought him a small sailboat.

Hank was gorgeous. Very tall and, like his mother and father, his arms and legs were the longest parts of his body. His skin turned brown from the sun and his hair turned straw yellow.

When he looked at you with his blue eyes, you could tell he was a special young man.

In high school he would hang around the fire station where he found his future. Eventually, he became a paramedic.

He gave his only girlfriend, Julie, a ring and then, on the drive back from a scuba diving trip in Florida with some of the other paramedics, he died.

He was 22 years old. The doctor told Laura it was due to a gene and that his heart had exploded.

I flew in from Michigan, my imagination filled with memories of Hank as a toddler running back and forth between me and his father on a marbled floor medical building at Turo Infirmary in New Orleans.

Laura wouldn't even attend those checkups, convinced her son was in no danger of a heart defect.

All the cousins gathered with our Aunt Laura, and Julie's family for the most devastating funeral imaginable. There was a short service at the funeral home in Bay St. Louis. Then all of us shared cars in a caravan for the drive to the cemetery in New Orleans where Uncle Harry was buried next to his mother. Hank was buried in the grave that was supposed to be for his mother.

Everyone thought Laura would fall apart. But her grief took her to a place of dead calm. All the rage and ambition, the denial she carried for so long, disappeared. She had to find a way to care for herself. She had before and she would do it again.

She was able to get a farm widow's loan from the Federal Government, so she built herself a nice, little, two-bedroom house.

All the furniture she and Harry had bought for their first house fit perfectly. About the same time the house that Laura built on the taxpayers' dime was completed, she bought three plots under a double trunk pine tree in the old Bay St. Louis cemetery. She made enough profit on the sale of the two plots in the New Orleans cemetery where Hank and Harry were buried, to move their caskets and markers to the new plots in Mississippi.

Aunt Billie, who saved nothing, was appalled that Laura would bother, and then she learned that the sale of the original plots also paid for a beautiful marker for Laura's gravesite.

Branches of dogwood blossoms surrounded her name. Billie couldn't understand why she even cared for a pretty marker, but Laura took care of business, even in her grief, which her sisters didn't understand. It was Laura's way of gathering the two men she most loved. It was an act of yielding. Something she had never been capable of achieving.

Her health steadily declined. She had seizures and after a bad fall, Aunt Billie decided it was time to take care of yet another sister in need. But this time she arrived with a sense of duty and without the love with which she joined forces with Mama.

For a while, she and Laura made out well together. Billie would drive them both to New Orleans to see Laura's dentist and have lunch and martinis at Pascal's Manale restaurant on Napoleon Avenue.

As time went by, they would go to one of the many new fish restaurants in nearby Gulf Port or Pass Christian. They got drunk at those lunches. I knew them. And I'm sure they laughed and had fun. Fun was the saving grace for both women. It helped them forget.

It was following one of those meals with martinis that finally did Laura in. She fell from the stairs of the restaurant onto the gravel parking lot and almost tore her face away.

By this time, Laura's ability to think clearly had already raised red flags. One day shortly before her fall, the sisters were at the Safeway. Near the check-out area, Laura pulled her pants down, squatted and urinated onto the floor splattering, not a few shocked patrons. Aunt Billie called and told me about it and was amazingly empathetic.

"I just went over to her and told her she needed to pull up her pants and not worry about toilet paper. She forgot where she was, and I don't think it even shamed her. She didn't know."

Billie had already begun to work at the insurance company for Laura. There was no office job Billie could not quickly learn. She resigned herself to work again after her retirement.

After Laura's fall, she spent several weeks in the hospital, just long enough for Ellen and Billie to begin the process of taking over Laura's affairs. They sold her house and used the little equity to move their older sister into a nursing home near Covington.

Billie found an apartment in Covington which was near Ellen and L.C. By that time she was free, her husband Scott, had died a few years before.

Aunt Ellen's grief over putting her older sister in a home was poignant. She made soft, flannel, pastel covers with crocheted lace around the borders for Laura.

Both sisters took turns visiting, they each went at least twice a week.

. . .

Ellen prepared delicate turkey sandwiches for her sister, cutting off the crust and mashing up homemade cranberry sauce into mayonnaise.

Billie would stop at the nearby Burger King and pick up a malted milk and hamburger. She also supplied Laura with cigarettes since the nursing home had a smoking room.

Whenever I drove in from Houston, I would take either Ellen's turkey sandwiches or Billie's cartons of cigarettes, always something that my aunts put into my hands for their sister.

The nursing home was clean, but not top dollar by any means. There were no carpeted floors or paper on the cement block walls, but Laura was treated gently by the staff, and she had a private room that was sunny. There was none of the usual smell of old urine that clung to many nursing homes of that era, and sadly, still does.

The smoking room, on the other hand, should have been demolished.

It was dark and smelled like an unbelievably bad AA meeting. It made my eyes water, but the natives were interesting, and Laura thought of them as the best friends she ever had, and they may have been.

They were an assortment of retired prostitutes, barmaids, and worn-out store clerks and someone's neglected mother. I remember there was one man, a regular. He had no legs, but he always proudly and loudly declared, "Look, God saved my hands so I can still smoke."

I had quit smoking some years before, but Laura would have me light up her cigarettes for her because of her terrible tremors. She would smile and tell the other women, "Watch, she's going to start smoking again. Look at her, light my cigarettes for me."

My cure from ever lighting up another cigarette took place over the course of visits to Aunt Laura.

I couldn't leave her without crying every time I told her goodbye. She would pat my hand and tell me, "Don't cry Jere, I'm fine."

She was. She had reached the final stage of acceptance and lost the need to reach for the elusive life of gentility and ease that she had expected would be her due after marrying Harry.

My godmother became a gentle spirit who died in peace.

Ted and I drove to Bay St. Louis for Laura's funeral.

The sisters had gotten a priest to come and say the prayers of the dead. The poor man didn't know any of the family, and certainly not Laura. I don't know if he didn't ask, or they didn't feel it was any of his business what happened in her life.

My cousin, Luddy's wife, Beth and I knelt together at Laura's coffin and made a whispered promise to ourselves and Laura that when Ellen and Billie died, we would take over the funeral arrangements and do it right.

But Billie could find no peace with Laura's death. Laura began to haunt her, and she felt an open hatred.

It was the haunt that kept me attuned to the shifts in Aunt Billie's psyche, a fancy word for soul. In some way, it was the combined soul of the four sisters who would lead me to the story I had spent my life seeking.

The first sense I had that Aunt Billie was going into dementia was her refusal to talk about the past, even the recent past.

Then in each succeeding visit, I would discover the lists.

Pages of lists in her neat, small, ever growing smaller handwriting like she was trying to save paper.

There was this compulsion to put everything she needed to

remember on one page for each day. Pages torn from small spiral notebooks and free notepads were neatly lined up, side by side, row after row, on the long countertop next to the phone.

There was a second bedroom in her garage apartment. She called it Jere's room. No one else from out of town visited her.

The closet of my room backed up against her room and was empty except for the metal hangers awaiting my clothes. As we prepared for bed, Billie said, "I hope Laura doesn't bother you."

"Billie, Laura's dead."

Billie said, "I know that. It's her ghost. Don't you hear her when you visit me?"

"No."

"I'm not crazy. I hear her moving around."

"Do you ever see her?"

"No, but I can sense she is in a hidden room somewhere behind my bed."

If ghosts in hidden rooms and the growing number of lists weren't an indicator of Billie's mental state, her driving provided the strongest clues.

Billie had always been an excellent driver. Long or short distances, she was a mindful and skilled driver. But in the last years before Katrina, I noticed some disturbing tendencies. She would drive down the middle of two-lane roads.

"People drive too fast. I don't want anyone to hit me. When I pull to the middle, it forces them to slow down."

She would slow to a near stop on a busy highway or street when she was approaching a grocery or restaurant parking lot.

One time when I was with her, she left the parking lot and went the wrong way on the adjourning street. When I pointed it out to her, she blew me off.

"It is easier this way. It takes too much time to go around."

I could almost understand her reasoning. The wrong way street was rarely used.

Finally, she began monitoring her driving by not going on freeways and limiting where she drove on the busy, two-lane Parish roads. None of us wanted to take away her keys, but soon Katrina would make that decision for us.

The month before Hurricane Katrina hit New Orleans in 2005, my husband and I stayed at a B&B on Delgado Street across from the rented duplex Julian and I shared with my mother's parents during WWII.

The whole duplex was vacant. In past years, I had driven by the house but never ventured up the driveway and into the backyard.

This time I brought old photographs of a tiny me sitting on the front steps and another from the same day of me squatting in front of a large, agave cactus plant on the side of the duplex. The steps and the cactus are still there. I walked around to the back of the house and was jolted by an experience of being brought back in time.

The backyard had not changed from my memory of it. The tin garage still sits at a right angle to the house next to the fenced-in key lot that is still Technicolor green with huge banana trees and elephant ears filling the lot.

The key lots held the outhouses before indoor plumbing. Well fertilized key lots are sometimes filled with squash and pole beans and tomato bushes. Some key lots have become neighborhood parks where neighbors gather sitting on shared furniture.

The driveway, and the yard of the duplex, and the one on its left are paved and a wooden staircase still climbs to a balcony with cross rails that overlook the pavement.

I had forgotten those boards until this minute. Mama always

said I fell off the balcony while riding my little bike. But there is no way a child could ride her tricycle off the balcony except by falling down the stairs. That is an enormous difference, a two-story fall straight down or a tumble down a flight of stairs.

For years, the mystery of the fall and injury haunted me. The suspicion that someone tried to kill me lurked in my mind. As I stood looking up at the staircase, I could see myself tumbling down the stairs. But the child behind the screen is faceless. Is this child behind the screen the part of me who observes and remembers the accident?

I remain terrified of stairs. I miss a step and fall, lacking the ability to stop myself. Did I, as a small child, panic, look up and out, and lurch forward?

The lurch becoming imbedded in my body's memory, felt now as a fear of heights, experienced as the fear I will fall, leap, be pushed, or pulled over the edge of a precipice.

My mother always said WWII made it so I did not scar badly. She said I reaped the benefits of those new sutures developed for wounded soldiers. She also told me I was alone when I fell. But I didn't believe her.

I was sure there was another person with me. Not my brother, he would have stopped me. But the scream gets in the way when I try to remember the face or the details of another person.

New memories, uninvited, enter my imagination. The blackout curtains become a metaphor for an unexamined memory.

A small, naked child is lying across someone's lap. The room is without light. I believed until now;, the memory was suggested by something else later, a movie or a wicked therapist. Now I realized the fall was a metaphor or lie Mama used to try and cover up a deeper hurt and the memory of the naked child was indeed me.

I remembered another day, blurred by time. The part that

remains clear is an interior moving picture of the young me pulling my tricycle up the back stairway toward the balcony that still hangs over the paved yard.

The screen door at the top of the stairs leads into the upstairs tenants' apartment. I am moving toward a child barely seen behind the screen. Then, I am riding my tricycle. I do not remember falling two stories down to the pavement. I do not remember the pain or the surgery that followed. Throughout my childhood, small scars mark my face. Scars time has faded from the naked eye.

These memories fill my mind as I look at the structures and the key lot of the old apartment I have not seen since my third year. How could that be?

Were those memories of the blackout curtains connected to my childhood facial scars?

A few days later, I left Ted and drove across the long Causeway that crosses Lake Ponchatrain and stayed in a hotel while I visited aunts and asked about the injuries I sustained in the fall during the War. They deny any knowledge of a fall or surgery.

"But don't you remember the scars on my face?"

Ellen assured me, "You were a tomboy. You always were cutting and scraping yourself."

Billie said for the hundredth time, "Your mother just let you children run wild."

I realized, as usual, when I brought up anything to do with their father or the apartment we lived in during the war and their mother's last days;, I was being held at bay and distracted from my quest. But I wanted to know the secret they carried about me.

Then Aunt Ellen asked the critical question.

"What happened to Mama' scrapbook?"

"I thought you had it. You sent me her purse filled with yellow stamps."

"She had it all packaged and ready to go. She put stamps all over it, so we could just drop it in a mailbox. She didn't trust Bob, and she knew she was dying."

"No, I didn't take anything out of that house. Not her umbrella or a scrap of paper."

I was crushed. I just wanted to go home.

The night after Katrina, August 30, 2005, I received a late-night call from my aunt Billie. Her voice was clear and to the point.

"Jere, come and get me. I don't know where I am."

Another voice came on the line, telling me my Catholic aunt had sought shelter in a Unitarian church in Baton Rouge. I knew right where it was as I had been doing research in a nearby library. I got the directions, so I didn't have to depend on memory, and told her to settle down for the night, I'd be there the next day.

The drive east from Houston along I-10 was so strange. Normally it was a four-to-five-hour trip to Baton Rouge, but that day it took a little over three hours. There was no traffic. No buses carrying refugees, no supply trucks, no road work. Just small groups of exhausted men carrying their old-fashioned cardboard suitcases or sitting on the curbs of gas stations and rest areas.

The landscape looked incredibly worn, or like a glimpse into some unknown future.

I drove, listening to Tom Waits and Lucinda Williams. Tom sings in his whiskey voice about missing New Orleans, and Lucinda, wails "Sweet Mama, I love you, Mama."

Driving east on I-10, singing along, crying, trying not to see what I am seeing and taking it all inside of me like bad air was overwhelming.

It was an exceedingly long day. Part of the problem was that a young cousin had moved Aunt Billie and her two traveling companions from the shelter to her small apartment located in student housing at LSU, which was the epicenter of all emergency outreach.

That little detour took over five hours in stand still traffic. To navigate through it I had to make sure Billie's friend could follow me for another five hours to the Mississippi River Bridge.

In Houston, during her six-week stay after the storm, Billie watches old movies and sits with her arms crossed when I turn on the news.

"Why do you want to watch that? It's too depressing."

"I have to see what's happening."

"I don't like to look at it. I have my beliefs."

"Do you ever find that your beliefs are undermined by what you see?"

"I don't see it. I have my beliefs."

My generous aunt Billie with her harsh beliefs simply condemns people to hell.

"I don't condemn them. God does that."

"But how do you know?"

"Because I read my Missal and say the Rosary and I keep up with the Fatima letters."

"But how do you know who will go to hell? Does God tell you?"

"I know what I know."

I make her go through a litany of the condemned, and the saved as I call out the names of her sisters and other people we know.

I screw up my courage.

"What about me?"

"I don't want to fight anymore."

"Do you pray for me?"

"I pray."

She has made a joke and doesn't allow herself to smile.

Forced to evacuate her apartment in Covington, she arrives at my home in Houston weak and confused.

Every night, I sit next to her on the edge of her bed and watch as she reenacts a ritual as old as memory.

Aunt Billie wears medals of Mary, the Mother of God, and small bundles of cloth held together with a safety pin. The cloth pieces are scapulars that hold relics believed to have touched the body of a saint. She wears them pinned to the strap of her bra. I ask her about their meaning.

"They are supposed to make it, so you won't go to hell."

"No matter what?"

"You have to lead a good life."

"Do you think you have?"

"Yes. I helped a lot of people, your mother, Scottie, Laura, the old people in the country, the hospital volunteers, the patients…"

"Then why wear them?"

"It can't hurt."

I know Billie has worn these pieces of cloth and small medals since at least my childhood. They did not save her from Katrina or two bad marriages.

With each passing year since the dementia set in, Billie's ability to finish a thought diminishes. She cannot answer a direct question. She begins to stutter. She tells me stories now about her father and when her mother got so sick.

"Daddy was always hugging me, and putting his hand on my breast, and …."

If I asked for clarification, offered sympathy, or tried to bring the subject up, she would struggle to speak.

Her body would grow rigid as I tried to reassure her, "It's OK. You don't have to talk about it."

But a blockage in her brain had sprung a leak and she could not seem to stop herself.

Out of the blue, she would say, "He was always hugging on me, sticking his tongue in my mouth."

Catching herself, she makes the signs of the three monkeys, hiding her eyes, ears, and holding her mouth shut.

How many times had I seen her do that over my lifetime? How many times have I ignored it? Or thought it was just a remnant from her school days and didn't keep track. What had we been talking about? Was it just with me, or was it when she and Mama were talking, and I walked into the room? How many times had I missed the clues?

Still in Houston, Billie wants to return to Louisiana. But there is no electricity in Covington, and I realize she cannot go back to live in her garage apartment.

My house was a two-story and my husband and I are afraid she'll fall on the stairs. She watches television and does small chores.

Every afternoon she chops the parsley and garlic finely, to go in our salad or on whatever meat or fish I'm cooking. Indeed, I cook a lot of lean ground beef because it is her favorite. The taste and essence of food has not left her. She loves the time we spend in the kitchen. So, do I.

When hurricane Rita hit Houston a month after Katrina, we did not evacuate.

Our children called and begged us to leave, but I knew our area of Houston was high and not likely to flood. I did not trust the city or state to organize such a major evacuation. Houston's population was in the millions, and I was not sure they could ever get people and cars off the roads.

Billie wanted the comfort of a bed and bathroom. None of us felt up to roughing it in a car for hours, perhaps days. I placed all the files that were important to me and Ted in plastic storage boxes in case a tree or limb fell on the house.

And because there are old glass windows in every room of our home, we sought other shelter.

My friend Pat and his partner Sergio owned a large, old house and ran it as a bed-and-breakfast. They had boarded up the windows and invited all of us to stay with them.

Aunt Billie and I cooked a big pot of red beans and steamed rice, and we brought all the fresh and frozen fruit in the house to add to the large dessert our hosts were planning.

At the old turn of the century B&B, the dining room table was filled with people. Among them was a guest who couldn't get a plane home and friends who lived close by and helped with the boarding up of windows. It was a delightful hurricane party, and everyone drank too much wine. Billie even had a martini.

The guys had fixed a guest room for all of us. We realized Billie couldn't climb the steep stairs, so a mattress was brought down. She and I settled down on the mattress. Ted got the room upstairs to himself. I kept a light on for Billie. Before she fell asleep, she turned to me and asked, "Were those queer boys?"

"Does it matter, Billie?"

"Just wondering." She had a funny smile on her face. I knew she was reminded of another party from some other time in her life.

"Were they?"

"Yes."

"Even Pat and Sergio?"

"Yes. Go to sleep Billie."

"Will they go to hell?"

"No! Stop this. Just listen to the wind."

That same night, two other elderly women Ted and I knew were burned to death on a bus carrying residents of a Houston nursing home to Dallas. They were stuck in traffic for hours and, just south of Dallas, the tires caught fire.

The residents sitting toward the back of the bus were trapped. Many of them were on oxygen or too weak to walk. I never told my aunt that hell was as close as the next thing to go terribly wrong, but I would soon discover she already knew about hell in the here and now.

Even though there was no cable television, and it wouldn't be for weeks, Billie still wanted to return to Covington. She had friends there and a nephew whose wife Beth would watch out for her.

Beth is a southern cousin to me, and she might as well have been a sister. Her husband was Aunt Ellen's only son. She found a small, assisted living residence near the old Abbey, where my father's parents and other relatives are buried.

Both Beth and I did our best to make the two-room apartment as nice as possible. We cleaned out her garage apartment and moved Billie's and some other pieces of furniture, which were a better fit, into the new place. It was arduous work, both emotionally and physically. The air was still filled with moisture, making us more uncomfortable.

Covington had changed since the storm. Thousands of the tall pines had fallen over, dragging their tap roots out of the ground like huge snakes.

The air was filled with the sound of the chainsaws and the sawdust from the cut trees. The infrastructure of Covington was never set up for the traffic that followed Katrina as the residents of New Orleans, and neighboring small towns, all the way to Mississippi, vied for the limited supplies the businesses in Covington had in stock or were able to bring in.

I can't tell this part of the story without telling the story of Beth, my cousin Lud and their family, which included six children, mostly teens and college age, with the tag along, younger William still in grade school. They stayed put during Katrina. All of them did.

Covington is north of Lake Ponchatrain and the damage to the town resulted from Katrina's high winds.

The storm didn't carry much rain, so there was no flooding. In New Orleans and the Mississippi Gulf Coast, Slidell flooding was caused by a storm surge and the breaking of New Orleans' already weakened levies.

The Katrina winds caused a huge pine tree to fall and cut my cousins' house in half. The next morning, they found that Aunt Ellen's house was covered in fallen trees that made a pic-up-sticks canopy. But this was no game.

No one could get to the house to check on the couple until they cut the trees away from the roof. I can't even imagine what that was like. Cutting through fallen trees to get to the house, and then, men and boys with chain saws climbing up the fallen trees, cutting and strategizing where to make the next cut so the weight of the trees didn't crush the elderly couple.

Then Covington's electricity was cut off because of fallen lines.

Ellen and L.C. were sent to Baton Rouge to stay with their daughter Lucy.

Meanwhile, Billie, her landlord and another woman drove to Baton Rouge with orders to call Jere. Lud stayed behind in Covington while Beth took the children and her mother to North Carolina.

A surgeon, Lud, knew he would be needed, and he was. After the tree that destroyed part of his house was gone, he finally got a roofer.

. . .

Beth and the children arrived home to a whole new onslaught: mosquitos.

Rainwater caught between the walls became a breeding ground for the tiny swamp pests. They awoke one night to the insects swarming and biting everyone everywhere. They covered themselves with sheets, trying to ward off the insects. But that did not work, even on a temporary basis. So, in the middle of the night, the whole family, eight strong, found tools and began tearing the sheetrock off the walls. All of this by candlelight in stupefying heat and humidity. It would take weeks for the electricity to be restored. It would take more months to repair the house.

It was hard to find carpenters or materials. On one of my visits, I found my young cousins, Forest and his younger brothers Elliot and William, helping their father hang the sheet rock on the walls and ceilings throughout the damaged parts of the house. They worked on Friday nights and all day on Saturdays.

Sunday mornings they all attended the Methodist Church on Jefferson Avenue, but by afternoon they were back on the ladders, tools in hand.

I remember one Sunday night my cousin Forest speaking for everyone as he raised his head off the kitchen table and out of his hands.

He looked exhausted.

"This is my senior year in high school. This is supposed to be my happiest year. I can't spend another weekend like this. I am too tired."

He did spend many more weekends working; they all did, because that is what it took to bring a new normalcy back into their lives and into the town.

. . .

I have finally written a book that brought me straight into the terror of finding out the truth behind the beautiful faces and memories of Mama and her sisters.

There is a photograph of the four Riggs girls that was taken at a studio in New Orleans in 1943. It was taken when we were all living in the apartment near City Park and their mother was dying.

I was three years old. I remember sitting on some small riser and watching the photographer. No matter where I have lived over the years since I moved into my own home, I have kept that photo in a special place.

Mama is dressed in her good, black, crêpe dress; a pearl pin secures the bodice so there is no chance of exposing her small breasts. But her raven hair hangs with abandon.

Laura, the tallest of the sisters, is dressed in black also, but with soft, white lace around her throat and down her breasts. A cameo pin attaches at the center of the lace, keeping it in place. Her hair is light brown and the short cut frames her long face.

Aunt Ellen is in the middle under Laura. She wears a dark dress with white dots; white lace around her neck, her blond hair hangs long and wavy.

Billie wears a simple, white blouse that hides her breasts, and her hair is in a long, perfect page boy. Her lips are full and ripe, but her eyes are already clouded as she pulls them ever so slightly toward the camera lens.

I thought it was a photo of young women who still had a chance, but now I realize they were already broken.

Their fates were sealed long before the four gathered around their dying mother. They always spoke of that time being so terrible. I never stopped to wonder why their mother's death wasn't a relief. Their mother had been ill for such a long time. I just assumed they loved their mother like I loved mine. I now realize they protected her.

· · ·

After years of living in apartments in the Carrolton Section of New Orleans, Aunt Ellen and L.C. bought a house off a block from the Streetcar line.

It was a lovely French Styled shotgun house with a long porch along the side that had French doors leading to the interior rooms. The kitchen and dining room were all the way to the back. The living room was all the way to the front with two large bedrooms between front and rear. Soaring ceilings, two front windows that opened and closed from bottom and top. These houses were built for the humid heat of New Orleans with ceiling and or attic fans to keep the air moving.

I remember my grandfather, Whoo Paw, visiting us when we lived on Military Road. I know he came the night Daddy went crazy, and I hid in the dark with baby Clay. There are photos of him at Ellen's house when her children were little. He spent every Christmas with them.

After we moved back to New Orleans in 1956, I saw him more frequently. By then, I thought of him as a role model of a good father. He seemed wise and kind. My aunts and mother led me to believe, his goodness was lifelong.

When I was sixteen, I remember sitting on his lap in Ellen's large living room while Mama and my aunts and uncle sat drinking from tall bourbon and coke glasses filled with ice, laughing, and talking about who knows what?

The whole while, Whoo Paw tells me I shouldn't smoke and then teaches me how to blow smoke rings. We got so good that we could blow rings through our separate rings, leaving a trail of smoke that rose toward the ceiling until the rings disappeared. I remember French inhaling through my nose and blowing the smoke rings out of my mouth. It was all in the tongue.

It was strange that these women who were so obsessive about my sexuality, who held this huge secret, would sit in Ellen's living room smoking, drinking their bourbons, laughing, and talking like it was perfectly normal and safe for a big girl in the fullness of her sexuality to sit on her grandfather's lap blowing smoke rings while he whispered stories from his time in WWI.

He was still in his late fifties. I remember his smell of hair oil and bay rum, mixed with bourbon and coke, and Camel cigarettes and the feel of his beard if I got too close to his face.

"They didn't train us right. It was hell to be in the infantry. None of us were prepared for the cold or the trenches. They were like ditches that were filled with rain. It rained every day and then it snowed, and the snow turned into ice and melted, making thick mud. The infantry marches in rain and mud mixed with snow."

Whoo Paw would stop talking long enough to light another cigarette before resuming his story. His voice was raspy from the lifelong habit of lighting one cigarette off a new one before the one he was smoking was fully finished. Then put out the old one in a full ashtray on the table next to our chair.

Uncle L.C. quietly shifting his attention away from the laughing women to his father-in-law when Whoo Paw began talking about WWI.

Aunt Ellen's husband served in the Army Air Corp in WWI in the huge bombers that were stationed in the Philippines.

"The city boys from the north who never hunted or fished a day in their lives wouldn't take off their boots or change their socks the whole time we were stuck in the trenches, sometimes weeks at a time."

Taking another swig from his drink and motioning to the younger children to bring us a new ashtray, he would slowly continue.

"By the end of the war, the boys who survived finally took off their boots. Their feet rotted so much they came right off with their boots." Snuffing out another cigarette and lighting another, Whoo Paw continued.

"They learned how to train soldiers for WWII from the mistakes on the feet of the infantry in WWI.

One time we had to cross the Rhine River, going hand over

hand along a rope stretched across the river. Out of two hundred of us, twenty made it across. Those city boys couldn't even swim. They let go out of terror and the numbing cold."

An older Julian reminds me of another story our grandfather told about the end of WWI.

Whoo Paw held the rank of Captain and commanded a small machine gun brigade. They were all Louisiana boys. As Julian tells it and I remember it, "When the German soldiers surrendered on Armistice Day, November 11, 1918, at the eleventh hour, our grandfather gave the order to his men to gun down the surrendering German troops."

Julian sees it as an act of cruelty. I see the cruelty and unlawfulness, but I also see it as an act of exhaustion. And perhaps even for southern boys and men, the rule of hate for all enemies. For me, the question remains, what did that act of murder do to our grandfather and his men? Did those Louisiana boys, who still carried the anger of defeat from the Civil War, ever feel remorse, or were they left only with the anger of denial?

CHAPTER 25
Flashback

CHAPTER 26

The Rhine River

[1998]

Four days after Aunt Laura's funeral in Bay St. Louis, Ted and I were on a train passing through Rotterdam on the way to Amsterdam.

I wanted our trip to Germany to start there partly because it was counterintuitive, the Rhine River flowed north from the Swiss Alps and emptied into the North Atlantic. I wanted to see the terrain and towns along the river my grandfather described as being frigid, with strong currents.

We had no hotel or pension reservations, and the train was late, so we just made it to the tourist office across from the huge terminal where drug deals were being made in the open.

To my amazement we were able to find a room in a house next to the famous Concertgebouw near the Museum Square. The house was four stories high and very narrow. We were on the top floor and had the most beautiful room of any of our trips. The large windows on the outside wall looked down on the shared patio with the concert hall.

. . .

Our first night at a bar near our pension was interesting, to say the least.

Everyone spoke excellent English and was friendly and welcoming until we revealed we were from Houston.

A Dutch tourist had recently been shot to death by a Texas homeowner. It was Halloween, and the tourist was wearing a mask as he was looking for a nearby party.

The homeowner was found innocent under a Texas statute that gives homeowners the right to protect their property – no questions asked. Everyone was sorry, but it was the law.

If the bar patrons and waiters expected us to defend the Texas law, they were disappointed. We agreed with their anger and their disagreement about the right for anyone to carry a gun or carelessly murder a stranger.

The first day we visited the Stedelijk, a museum of modern and contemporary art.

My plan from the first planning of the trip was to follow the Rhine upriver toward the Swiss Alps. It was a shock to see a contemporary antiwar installation at this museum in Amsterdam.

The first room was filled with large blown-up photographs of war. There were photos from Vietnam, African and Mid-Eastern wars, as well as the killings in Serbia. As I turned, I faced a large wall photograph of a Texas paintball war. I recognized former neighbors from our first Houston suburb dressed in battle fatigues and vests hiding behind trees and staring into the camera.

In one cell the doors imprisoned stacks of books. Already there were parents across the United States insisting on the removal of books from school libraries.

In another, the installation was simple. Old army boots were suspended from the ceiling by wires. The movement of people through the room caused the boot to march much like a ghost platoon.

I had entered a visual representation of my grandfather's description of soldiers in WWI whose feet had rotted off their bodies when they removed their boots. I realized it was a true memory and that new shadow soldiers still march to the rhythm of our breath as it set the mood for our excursion up the Rhine River to the Swiss Alps.

On our last day, we visited the Ann Frank Museum located in the area where the Frank family and others had sought refuge from the German Army during WWII.

Like so many other women who connected to the story and the little girl who wrote about her adolescence hiding in these rooms during the changes her body was making so that she could one day bear her own children and fulfill her sexual yearnings I climbed those stairs that rose like a ladder.

All of us were part of a pilgrimage to our own hidden lives during the early days of puberty and beyond. As well as our life-long rejection of hatred.

Amsterdam set the stage for what would become an exploration of war.

In Paris there were markers that read, "Ici, here on this spot the gestapo arrested and killed Pierre Margarite...."

Traveling throughout Germany there were plagues and the newness of old cities that had been rebuilt after the Allied bombings. I was struck by the impatience of the German people we met on our travels. I realized they could not forget the bombings and the war America won.

Even as I recognized my own dislike for these people with their love for afternoon sweets and sherry and beer gardens at night and the stores and businesses that no longer had Jewish names, I had expected they would be friendly and greet us with open arms.

For the first time, I knew what it felt like to be a conqueror. And so, following the Rhine River by train, mile by mile, we made it to the Swiss Alps.

When I was seventeen, Mama and Billie allowed me to visit my grandfather in Long Beach, Mississippi.

I stayed with his brother, and sister-in-law, Uncle Tot, and Aunt Helen. Tot drove me to the dock in Gulf Port to meet my grandfather early on a Saturday morning.

The tour boat took us to Sea Island, a small sand drift piece of land far enough out into the Gulf to reside in clear water. As we sat on the peer waiting for the ferry, Whoo Paw pointed into the water and told me about the large Stingrays swimming around the dock while we sat on the bench near the rail. I was terrified of the large flat black bodies of the fish and the danger from their hook tails. But I wouldn't let on to my grandfather my fear of their hooks.

I wore a sun dress over my swimsuit. I had a towel. I remember that. And some tap water in an old mayonnaise jar that Helen had given me. The waters near the beaches of the Mississippi coast were brown and muddy from the silt of the Mississippi River that dumped into the Gulf.

The water off the Island was clear blue and fish, and crabs were visible to the naked eye. I played and swam in the water and soon forgot my fear of what else was in the water with me. When the horn sounded for the return trip to the Gulp Port, my grandfather walked over a nearby dune carrying an arm load of grass.

On the trip back to the mainland, Whoo Paw named each kind of grass.

Years later, I would remember the image of my grandfather walking over the dune and write about that day and my realization that this man was one of my human images of God. He was a naturalist, raising hundreds of Camila bushes.

On previous visits with my mother and Aunt Billie, he showed me how to cut into a stem at an angle, placing another specimen's stem with flower into the slit, bounding them with green florist tape.

After his wife died in the early forties, he spent his last year living with his adopted sister, and mother. Both women were unhappy, his mother living in her wheelchair, and his sister, Aunt Patsy, who was tired of taking care of the old woman who had her own brand of abandonment.

When the boat docked back in Gulf Port, Whoo Paw put me on a beach bus and told me where to get off so I could make my way back to Uncle Tot and Helen's home across from the Gulf Road.

I got off the bus too soon and had to walk several miles in the dark along the beach to get back to my hosts. Sunburned, dehydrated, and exhausted, it was after eleven at night before I made my way to their house.

Helen was furious with my grandfather for not riding with me. Then she said something like, "Everyone knows that man…"

Tot shushed her, and it grew noticeably quiet. During the night, I had a nightmare that woke everyone up with my screams. The dream was about a woman in a toga dress standing on a platform between tall columns, and everything in the dream was blue.

I had no idea why the image was so terrifying, but in the morning, I insisted on going back to New Orleans.

Uncle Tot drove me to the Greyhound station, telling me the whole way Helen didn't mean anything, she was just upset.

When Mama and Billie picked me up, they didn't question me. Billie was upset because it was a waste of money, but I never told them about the dream or what Helen said that night, because

I forgot what was said as soon as I entered the bus and headed for home.

But I had a memory, one I couldn't be sure was true, of a man touching me in the dark bedroom where my brother and mother slept. The image would come and go. I worried I made it up as I was pulling pieces of the past together. And the color blue of that terrifying dream, returned in waves of color, but in my later years it was a comforting color that I could bring up as I sought to heal myself and my mother and aunts from the hurts of our childhood.

CHAPTER 27

The Eclipse

[2007]

Aunt Billie takes another fall and has to go into the hospital. She is unable to complete a sentence. On her release, I move her back into her small, assisted living apartment and sleep on the sofa.

The first night, neither of us gets much sleep. She is confused and I discover she is curled into a ball, sure she cannot breathe, but I determine her stomach is upset and take her to the bathroom.

As the hours roll by, I find her sitting on the side of the bed, her head held in her hands. She shakes her head if I inquire or try to offer comfort. I bring her trays of food and sit with her while she eats.

We walk outside a bit. She makes it to the dining hall. Gradually, in a matter of a few days, her strength and orientation make a slow return as she begins talking about her daddy.

It is the same old memories of her father touching and kissing her that I thought were mere manifestations of his loneliness and grief over his dying wife. But I have caught on, and I do not question. I just listen for the sound of her voice. It is as if she is talking in her sleep. Maybe when I'm not there, she talks to her dead sister Laura.

I realize then Laura has followed her to her new home. Laura now surrounds Billie. She confuses me for Laura, like she used to confuse me for my mother. Then I realize she knows exactly who I am. I am little Jere, all grown up, and she wants *me* to know something. I have finally become *me*.

I don't know why it has taken me so long to do what I know I must do. I am afraid. Have I waited too long? What good can come from asking the question burning inside of me? I don't want to hurt anyone. They're so old, so helpless. I feel mean. And then I ask myself, why am I here? I am a faithful person, but that is not why I visit and stay with my Aunt Billie, listen to her, try to talk to a crazy, old woman who is not anyone I know anymore. I have been stalking a town that is more interesting in memory than reality. But now I know what attracts me to this place.

I take a side trip to visit my grandmother Nonnie's grave.

The day before, a Saturday, I had gone to the farmers' market and bought two succulents commonly known as hens and chicks, taking its name from its manner of propagation.

If you take a leaf off the mother plant and put it into a bit of dirt, then lovely, new, tiny plants sprout. I had planned to give one as a gift and bring another one home with me. I only thought of them as I gathered the blanket to take with me. Only then did I take the spoon.

I drive to the Abbey. The cemetery is past the large church filled with paintings that seem to pop out of the mud-colored walls. Painted by a Dutch Monk during the seventies, Aunt Ellen calls them the work of the devil. I doubt she has even seen them, though many in the town agree with her. They are beautiful, moving images.

. . .

Back in my car, I drive down the driveway to the cemetery. It takes me a while to find my grandmother's grave. I seem to have developed this habit of losing graves, even when I have often visited them. I must wander around for a bit until I am forced to call out to the dead.

"Where are you?"

Finally, the dead respond.

"Stop! Look down. Here I am."

It is a game, I think, calling out to the dead, as I spread out a blanket I brought from home.

I sit on my grandmother's grave and read to her from the chapter about her teaching me about death.

I find a snake hole next to the plaque that reads *Rachel Linton Smith*. I take the kitchen spoon and begin to dig into that hole to widen it. I bury a leaf from the mother plant and cover it with the earth that surrounds the margins of the grave. I look around to the nearby landscaping; everywhere there are groupings of bushes and native trees. I bury more pieces of the mother plant just in case it takes root, and the groundskeeper lets it alone.

It was sunny and cold as I spread out the quilt on top of her grave as I tell Nonnie what I planned to do. I tell her how afraid I was to break through the world of privacy my aunts had built around anything to do with their childhoods. I tell her about Billie's dementia and Aunt Ellen's Parkinson's disease. Then I pray to Nonnie to help me put aside my aunts' illnesses and grant me the strength to break both their and my barriers to releasing their tongues. Finally, I pray to my Nonnie that I do it right, that I don't mess it up.

Satisfied I made all the proper rituals for breaking through barriers without hurting them, I drove to Ellen's house.

It was about two in the afternoon, and she was still in bed. She was awake and dressed in a beautiful, pink, satin nightgown. Her body was wasted from the effects of the disease and the disruptions caused by Katrina.

Uncle L.C. was still her main caregiver, and like so many men, he didn't want any strangers in the house. I found him asleep in his chair with the television turned to a baseball game. And for once, Ellen was alone.

Her voice had little volume, so I get into bed with her. Holding my face close to her lips, I say, "Ellen, Billie has been telling me stories about your father." I didn't know what to expect. Was she going to kick me out of her bed?

She didn't ask me any questions or hesitate as she told me the story of her childhood and adolescence. A retired nurse, she was almost clinical in her descriptions of her father's sexual behavior.

"He took me fishing and after a while, he opened his pants and took out his penis and masturbated right there in front of me."

"How old were you?"

"I was twelve, and I didn't have words to describe what I was seeing, so I couldn't tell anyone. He was my father, and I loved him so much. Over time he showed me how to masturbate myself. He did other things. And I knew it was wrong, but I couldn't tell anyone."

"What about teachers?"

"I couldn't tell them something like that."

"Didn't your sisters talk to you? They must have known."

"They were gone, and I couldn't tell mother."

"Ellen, how long did he do this?"

"When I was seventeen, I started dating and began to understand. I told him it was wrong, and we couldn't do that anymore."

"Do you think he did this or some variation with your sisters?"

"I know he didn't do it to Laura. He was the one to discover her stomach was bruised and seeped blood. He took her to the doctor, and it was discovered the hymen covered her whole vagina and her menstrual blood was backing up, into her abdomen."

"I remember hearing that story. I thought he was such a good father to take her to a doctor, particularly about a female problem. Now it takes on a whole new meaning."

"He was a good father. He had this thing, but don't ever tell or write that he was a bad father or a bad man."

Then I asked, "Is *that thing* about your father why all of you were so vigilant about my sexuality? I always thought you all knew some terrible thing about me. That I was somehow intrinsically vile? Do you know where that came from?"

"We all tried to protect you. You were such an extroverted and cute little girl."

"I know. I've seen the photos. Did I seem overly promiscuous to you all?"

Instead of an answer, Ellen changed the subject.

"We tried to protect you from your father because he was unpredictable when he was drunk."

"He was that, but Mama let me go to bars with him. I spent hours sitting on barstools and dancing on Mr. Tugy's bar and later at other bars." I tried not to show my increasing anger.

Bringing her back to her own father, I said, "Ellen, I have an image from the time we lived in the duplex during the war. I'm in a dark room, the blackout curtains are closed and I'm lying naked over someone's lap, and they hurt me. And I'm crying and they slap me, spank me. I don't know if it is a true memory or imaginary."

"It probably is a real memory. You were very constipated when you were in New Orleans. Someone was inserting a suppository."

Why didn't I think of that? I didn't believe her either, but I didn't want her to stop talking to me. I was afraid to push too much because I wanted to understand, or at least learn, as much as possible. I knew enough to not allow myself to stop her with too many questions.

Sitting side by side, Aunt Ellen and I talked for a long time. She talked about her mother and how they had never had a lovely home and how poor and sad they all were. She said that during high school, when her older sisters were gone, she and her parents lived in a single room of a rooming house in Bay St. Louis.

"Do you have any idea what that was like? Never being able to invite a friend to my home?"

I did understand. I know that part of it was I had to watch out for Clay, and Julian was studying at Tulane, and he demanded privacy when he was home. And part of it was I liked to be alone. Home was a refuge.

"Aunt Billie, I talked to Ellen." Billie didn't blink or look away from me. She stayed steady for the whole conversation.

"What'd she say?"

"She told me her daddy would take her fishing, starting when she was twelve. He would unzip his pants and masturbate in front of her. He did other things. She said she never told anyone. She said there was nobody to tell. She couldn't even tell her own mother."

"No, she couldn't tell Mother."

"Billie, I always thought that from things you said, about your father sticking his tongue in your mouth and touching your breast, it was something that started during WWII when you were all beautiful, young women, and your mother was so sick. But she was sick all the time, even when you were children."

I didn't know how much I could ask or tell her. I waited for her to speak.

"We decided it was in the past. And we never talked about it again."

"Billie, you all made him a hero." She became rigid.

"He was no hero! We tolerated him because of mother."

"What about me, Billie? Why did you all let him near me when I was little?"

"He wouldn't hurt you."

"How do you know that?"

"He just wouldn't. We never left you alone with him."

It was true. I don't remember being alone with my grandfather.

When I was little and we lived in New Orleans during WWII, I remember riding horsey on his leg.

Everyone gathered in the evening to have their bourbon and coke over ice chipped from a large block in the icebox that kept my milk cold.

I remember he would save the last dregs of his drink for me and the sweet pungent taste as I struggled to gather the smaller chips of ice into my mouth. But some nights, the sisters all went out on dates or to the USO dances. I was left alone.

What worries me is, I have no memory of what happened to me, and Julian would have been too young to protect me or even know I needed protection from our grandfather.

The four sisters built a wall around their childhood to protect the secret of their father's abuse.

My mother made up pretty stories about their childhood poverty, but the rest of the sisters rarely gave me information unless I had already found out something from someone else.

I remember fragments of that apartment in New Orleans during the war: the bare bones of ugly furniture, the iron beds in the second bedroom, contrasted with the beauty of the furniture my mother brought from Covington so her mother could die in a beautiful room.

I remember the sounds of my grandmother coughing and the

blue veins in her thin hands. I remember looking into the back of the radio set up in our dining room and searching for the little room in the back where Baby Snooks lived. I was only three years old.

That Sunday night while Billie slept, I drove into town. As I filled my gas tank, I saw that the full moon was in eclipse.

I had dinner and a double martini at an excellent restaurant that served my favorite, spicy, eggplant, stuffed with shrimp. With a full stomach, I slowly drove past all the houses I had lived in or visited during my childhood. I drove past the Catholic Church, St. Peters, and saw several cars parked.

The congregation had built a small Adoration Chapel in the area where we used to park our cars on Sundays.

I imagined that people who had lost their homes or loved ones in the hurricane were inside praying. I was reminded of when I was ten years old and trying to adjust myself to my parent's divorce, walking past the church, feeling a strange loss, and freedom as I looked forward to our new adventure in the west. And now, I felt so unbelievably free. I now knew I had been bound in chains for years. Finally, with one sentence, the silence of constraint was ended.

I parked my car and entered the chapel. The ornate monstrance that held a large host behind a glass door sat on a beautiful, quite simple antique standing desk or chest. Comfortable chairs were set around the room along with several kneelers.

I began to feel the pain of the people who were in prayer, grieving their losses. A metallic smell filled my nose. I recognized it as the smell of sweat on the rosaries people held in their hands. Rosaries passed down from one generation to the next, held in hands of the deepest sadness and grief.

I recognized anger seeping up through me as I gazed at the

monstrance, which was supposed to reveal the Son, Jesus, as a shining sun. But I recognized it as the glow of a full moon.

I remembered all the ways these women I loved, Mama, Laura, Billie, Ellen, did everything in their power to make me feel bad about my body in the name of protection.

I remembered the assault in my early teens and how Mama and Aunt Billie punished me instead of recognizing that they were doubling down on my hurt. It was their way of protecting me from the desires of any man I might encounter. I realized, under the glow of the moon goddess inside this chapel, that the inveterate wound I felt was their wound and mine to heal.

Telling the secret seemed to free my aunts. Soon after, Ellen moved into a nursing home and her body went through a period of rejuvenation. She became like a teenager discovering her newfound freedom. She dressed up every day, painting her lips red and flying down the hallways in her self-propelled wheelchair.

L.C. missed her terribly and one night he fell and broke his thighbone. He never walked again. Is this not biblical?

They had separate rooms in a new nursing home and took their meals together in the dining room for people with disabilities. They visited throughout the day, sharing their stacks of chocolate candy. And even though the secret was not his, somehow, he was freed also, no longer trying to control his wife.

I now believe that on that Sunday, when Ellen told me about her father, L.C. listened to our conversation on the monitor next to her bed. In my last visits with him, he seemed almost happy as we talked about his years in the Philippines during WWII, telling stories I had never heard until those last visits.

As for Billie, her speech was freed up when she did not have to guard her tongue any longer. She could hold eye contact throughout a conversation.

During Billie's period of renewed interest in life, I drove her to Bay St. Louis so she could see what she only imagined and worried about, like coffins rising out of the earth.

As we drove old Highway 90 into the Bay area, all the stores were destroyed or abandoned. I had to drive through back streets to get to the Bay. All my life the Bay Road drive was beautiful, even after the myriad of hurricanes.

Many of the houses were quite old, with porches and protected sunrooms, and old servant quarters that were turned into guest houses for the ever-expanding families and paying guests.

The yards and grounds were filled with huge oak trees and tall pines, antique azalea, and camellia bushes.

In the eighties, young families who worked in the space industry built newer houses in the pines behind the old homes, all the way back to the railroad tracks.

We could see the old bridge that connected the other gulf towns, Long Beach, Gulf Port and Biloxi, to Bay St. Louis, had been destroyed by the storm's powerful surge and winds.

We looked for all the homes along the bay that Billie and her sisters had lived in or visited. All gone.

Foundations and broken oak trees with white plastic material blowing like ghosts from the left behind trash were all that remained. From the Bay to the railroad tracks, nothing livable remained except for the mosquitoes.

Trees and houses were gone or so broken they would have to be removed and put into wood-chipper machines.

Across the tracks in Waveland, we found Billie's gravesite next to her husband's grave. Her worries about coffins floating up and out of the ground were proven false. The ridge supporting the tracks served as a levee, protecting everything behind it.

Then we drove to Laura's cemetery on the Bay side of the tracks. It had been a beautiful old cemetery with trees, reminiscent of a forest with its tall, long needle pines and old oaks that provided filtered light.

Over my godmother's grave, chosen so carefully by her with her son and husband on either side, was the lone surviving tree. It was shaped like a giant tuning fork, its branches stripped away. But the coffins remained beneath the ground.

I had packed a picnic lunch, thinking we might sit among the dead. But because of the mosquitos, Billie and I sat in the car to eat with a tablecloth covering our bodies.

It was peaceful, and we were quiet and relaxed. It reminded me of our car trip long ago to Santa Fe when Billie and Mother fixed sandwiches on the hood of the red Studebaker Convertible and we all ate our meals inside the car.

"Don't you hear the ghosts?" Billie asked.

"I hear the workers on the train tracks."

"Not that. The ghosts!" She was emphatic.

There was a sound. It rose in pitch, becoming surreal. It grew like the whistle of a steam engine.

Who knows? Perhaps we were hearing the ghosts of dead trees, and washed away beaches, of destroyed buildings and homes, lost lives, and bridges that no longer connected land to land, or of cloudy memories and lost souls.

The sound was that loud.

Gradually, Billie's body began to fail, and she could no longer care for herself.

As a retired government worker, her income was too high for Medicaid, so we moved her to a nursing home close to Beth's home. Her savings were almost gone, and Beth and I were worried about how we were going to handle the issues that would bring.

When I told Clay he began to send me $500 a month, most of which I was able to save and return to my bachelor brother. True to the patterns of her long life, Aunt Billie would die before she ran out of money.

In 2007, I drove back to Covington to spend Thanksgiving with her and family at Beth's home.

Billie refused to join us for dinner, blaming her stomach. But it really wasn't out of character, she had become a recluse. She liked to have visitors but drew the line at having to take advantage of the noise of large groups. She was always calm when I came to say goodbye, but this time was different.

She was in the hallway waiting for me and she couldn't speak. I realized she was holding back tears. I rolled her to her room, sat on her bed, and held both of her hands. I could tell she wanted to say goodbye but could not bring herself to say the words.

"Billie, I have to leave tomorrow, but I don't think I'm going to see you again."

"I hope not, but I don't know how to die."

"Sure, you do. It's easy. Just turn your back on the world."

Those words escaped out of me. I told her how much I loved her. And how grateful my brothers and I were for the way she came to us when Mama was so sick and afraid. We had already had that talk, but I wanted her to hear words of gratitude one more time. I was able to say goodbye and hold her one last time.

This complex woman who gave up her youth to take care of her sister's children helped me see with wide-open eyes even when she struggled to keep hers closed. I held her in my arms until she pushed me away and told me, "Go home. Don't worry about me."

Shortly after I returned to Houston, my Aunt Billie did turn her back to the world. Billie died right before Christmas in 2007. She was grateful and polite to her caregivers but ate and drank too little to sustain her life.

Beth called shortly after her death to report that Aunt Billie's face glowed in death and her wrinkles disappeared, so she looked young again. Beth could see the physical beauty of my young aunt I had told her about. I knew my search for the long-held secret of her father's betrayal had helped her find her glow just as it helped me find mine.

We all got to have our Christmas at our own homes. Billie had taken out a burial policy and wanted to be cremated.

Beth included her bundle of cloth, scapulars, and holy metals in the box her remains would be burned in. Her urn looked like a tabernacle; all heavy metal with a cross.

I delivered the eulogy, and Ellen said it was so good, I could deliver hers. The following summer, I made good on my promise.

After Billie's funeral luncheon, Beth and I drove the tabernacle of ashes to the Waveland cemetery and met Larry the grave digger.

It had been my job to arrange for the burial in a town that still had no infrastructure. There was no longer a board for the Waveland Cemetery, so on the sly, I was given the name of the gravedigger, Larry, by an unnamed official.

Larry met us near her grave site and dug a three cubic foot hole and as he lowered the metal box into the ground, Beth and I looked at each other and then at Larry. We had been so busy with the funeral service and the meal we hadn't planned on what kind of service we would provide at the gravesite.

We had brought red roses from the memorial service and began sprinkling them into the grave as Larry filled it with the sandy soil. Then we said one Hail Mary together, finally laughing as we hugged.

We had fulfilled a vow made at Aunt Laura's funeral when the exhausted sisters couldn't seem to find their way to making it special and the priest could not remember her name.

Our promise, made as we knelt at Laura's coffin, was to make sure Ellen and Billie had good funerals. Then we drove to Laura's cemetery, where we placed another bouquet of red roses on Laura's grave and knelt to say one last Hail Mary.

Of course, being us, we told Laura all about Billie's burial. We two women, one a devout Methodist, the other not much of anything anymore except a keeper of all things holy that the dead leave behind.

Epilogue

If you got this far, or like a lot of folks I know, read the intro and skipped to the last page, well maybe you'll stick around and read the middle part.

I have a few loose ends to tie into a bow. Throughout this book I have been calling my mother, Mama. When I was a child, I called her that one time which caused her to slap my face hard and tell me in her most demanding voice, that she was my Mother. And mama was a disrespectful and a country Yankee sounding name.

On a sadder note, my little sister, Cindi Loar passed away recently. She was 72 and died of heart failure, surrounded by family.

I had been writing about her and how I had to shake off all the old nonsense about not calling her my sister but only half-sister. We both had large families, and we had lost touch but she was still in thought obviously.

My son, Phil, drove us to Lake Charles for the funeral. I was so glad to see my nieces and brother-in-law, who called me from the hospital shortly before her death.

I do not let the dead go easily. And as my aunts died and were buried, I had a longing to bring my mother's remains back to the

Bogue Falaya River. I even called the cemetery in Washington, D.C. and inquired about the possibility. The man I spoke with was rather sarcastic.

He asked what I would bring to carry her home. A garbage can? My practical side overrode my want and so I wrote a play instead.

I already said I talk a lot to myself but in truth, I am mostly talking to God. He and I have a lot to say. Though, S/He is quiet, and just listens as I talk back to myself.

Mama not so much. When I told her I was going to burn her remains and the box I carried her in, and that the church had changed their rule on cremation I imagined our conversation on a stage.

Mama saying, "Why? I'm already dead. They can't do that, I'll never rise and go to heaven."

"Think about it, Mama. If your bones rot and you can still rise from the dead or come back at the end of time with all the other saints, why can't you come back if you turn to ash? People die in fires every day. Burned to a crisp. A few teeth and bits of bone. Pause. Am I disturbing you? Sometimes I do that to people."

"Honey, why do you want to bring me back to that?" I had told her about the storm.

"Mama, I want your spirit there. I want to make a little gris gris magic. I want to re-fertilize the river and the land with your ashes. Ashes to ashes, maybe it will bring about new life. You'll be home Mama, not with a bunch of strangers. I'll bring you to the river you loved. The Bogue Falaya. The place you went to when you needed something, where your wildness could be let free, and where you saved the woman from drowning."

" I don't need that."

"But I do. I need it. I need to dig you up, return you to Louisiana so then I can leave it and you behind.

I won't always be going back home feeling unfinished. I need to be free too. Mama, don't tell me what you don't need. Tell me if you would like to go back to the river."

We're both quiet standing in front of each other. I Exit. Curtain.

The End.

About the Author

Jere Pfister is a writer, storyteller, and truth-seeker who has captivated audiences on stages and in art galleries across Houston, Okemos Michigan, and Kansas City. Raised in the Jim Crow South in New Orleans, her natural curiosity led her to question and ultimately reject the rules and customs of her birthplace—a rebellion that would become the foundation of her lifelong quest for authenticity.

Pfister writes and tells stories of people and places where the tension of opposites collide: truth and lies, silence and revelation, shame and liberation. Her work explores the complex landscape of family secrets, religious hypocrisy, and the courage required to live authentically in a world built on beautiful deceptions.

With an MFA in Theater from the University of Houston, Pfister brings both dramatic sensibility and raw honesty to her storytelling. *Like a Fish Denied a River* marks her transition from performing truth on stages to excavating it on the page—a deeply personal memoir that chronicles her journey from a child crying out to God over dead pets to a woman bold enough to tell her most difficult truths to audiences, therapists, friends, famous playwrights, and most importantly, to herself.

Thank You for Reading
Like a Fish Denied a River
by JERE PFISTER

If you enjoyed reading this book, please consider leaving a review on your preferred platform. Your feedback supports quality content and helps inspire future releases.

Connect with the Author
jerepfister.com

Looking for Your Next Great Read?
Browse our Complete Catalog
brooklynwriterspress.com